*P*rivate *W*ealth

P9-CDL-069

RUSS ALAN PRINCE ○ HANNAH SHAW GROVE
CARLO A. SCISSURA ○ FRANK W. SENECO

MAXIMIZING
PERSONAL
WEALTH

An Advanced
Planning Primer for
Successful Business Owners

Charter Financial Publishing Network
499 Broad Street, Suite 120
Shrewsbury, NJ 07702

Maximizing Personal Wealth
An Advanced Planning Primer for Successful Business Owners
by Russ Alan Prince, Hannah Shaw Grove, Carlo A. Scissura, Frank W. Seneco

Copyright © 2015 by R.A. Prince & Associates, Inc. All rights reserved.

No part of this publication may be reproduced or retransmitted in any form or by any means, including, but not limited to, electronic, mechanical, photocopying, recording, or any information storage or retrieval system, without prior written permission of the publisher or copyright holder. Unauthorized copying may subject violators to criminal penalties, as well as liability for substantial monetary damages up to $100,000 per infringement, costs and attorney's fees.

This book is designed to provide accurate and authoritative information on the subject matter covered. This publication is sold with the understanding that neither the publisher nor the authors are engaged in rendering legal, medical, accounting, financial or other professional service or advice in specific situations set forth herein. Although prepared by professionals, this publication should not be utilized as a substitute for professional advice in specific situations. If legal, medical, accounting, financial or other professional advice is required, the services of the appropriate professional should be sought. Neither the authors nor the publisher may be held liable for any misuse or misinterpretation of the information in this publication. All information provided is believed and intended to be reliable, but accuracy cannot be guaranteed by the authors or the publisher.

Design: Martine Cameau | cameaudesign.com

To Jerry,
I am very impressed and very,
very proud of you.
Love,
DAD

For the openings, to JRF

HANNAH

To my mom, Teresa, who exemplifies
the true immigrant story, and to the
people of Brooklyn, who give me
inspiration each day...

CARLO

To my children, Stephanie and Alex, who are so dear to me.
Your love and affection mean the world to me and gives
me a purpose to keep striving forward and never give up.
And to my mother, Naomi Seneco, who raised me and
taught me the values that made me the person I am today.

FRANK

TABLE OF CONTENTS

FOREWORD

I am a passionate advocate for small businesses, because when they succeed there is an undeniable halo effect that helps strengthen the people and communities around them. This effect also manifests itself in the form of economic development, which is a hallmark of the US capital markets and essential to creating a promising future for Americans.

One of my responsibilities as the chairperson for the Committee on Small Business for the New York City Council is to increase access to the tools and resources that support and accelerate small business growth. I was immediately intrigued when I learned about the ongoing collaboration between Russ, Hannah, Carlo and Frank—four vastly different, but highly complementary professionals who have pooled their collective experience, wisdom, and networks—to help business owners enhance and protect the hard-earned value of their enterprises.

One byproduct of their efforts is the book you hold in your hands. *Maximizing Personal Wealth* includes timely and exclusive research on the needs of small business owners, a helpful guide on how to avoid the most common oversights and mistakes that lead to wealth erosion and destruction, and technical insights from some of the tri-state area's very best tax, accounting and legal experts on matters of business succession, advanced planning, and tax mitigation.

This book contains valuable and long-overdue information that can benefit all types of business owners, whether you are a first-time entrepreneur, the proprietor of an established company, or somewhere in between. I encourage business leaders and stakeholders to take advantage of this important and powerful resource that can result in stronger, smarter, and more successful businesses everywhere!

Robert E. Cornegy, Jr.
Chair, Committee on Small Business
The New York City Council

ABOUT THIS BOOK

Privately held businesses play an incomparably important role in the world's financial systems. As providers of goods and services, as taxpayers and as employers, they are the biggest driver of the global economy. At the same time, they are the biggest and best source of personal wealth creation. It's simply impossible to imagine what society would be like without them.

And given the recent surge of start-ups (and interest in start-ups), fueled by digital natives and the distribution power of the Internet, owning a privately-held business is likely to be one of the most exciting, impactful, and lucrative opportunities available to enterprising people now and moving forward.

The projected growth in the private sector was a key factor in the creation of this book. Over the past few decades, we have worked with and observed a wide variety of business owners allowing us to witness first-hand the activities that are most effective and those that are best avoided. When it comes to wealth creation and wealth preservation, most business owners make the same mistakes regardless of their age, gender, education, industry, or level of experience. They devote years to building a successful enterprise only to cede a significant portion of their income and net worth to unnecessary taxes, unfounded lawsuits, and unexpected circumstances. In short, we have witnessed billions of dollars in equity demolished by a lack of preparation and planning on the parts of business owners around the world.

Our work has also given us extensive exposure to high-net-worth individuals and the unique ecosystem of professionals and disciplines they rely on to sustain and enhance their fortunes. Advanced planning is one of those disciplines, a niche specialization that capitalizes on the tax code and the regulatory environment to protect and enhance hard-earned wealth.

The goal was to create an introductory resource for all business owners—especially those with substantial and thriving companies who may be considering succession options or a monetization event—that illustrates the lifecycle of equity-driven wealth creation and the actions you can take along the way to maximize your personal wealth. Each of its five sections contains the critical insights and guidance needed to navigate the process for the greatest financial results.

○ *Part I: Creating Personal Wealth* explores the mindset, characteristics, and approaches used by self-made millionaires that can amplify your business efforts.

○ *Part II: Advanced Planning* examines the typical lack of tax, estate, and asset protection planning among business owners and how a thoughtful, innovative, and ongoing process involving experts can reduce pointless loss and risk.

○ *Part III: Selected Strategies* discusses some approaches to business continuity and succession along with ways to mitigate income, estate, and capital gains taxes and build meaningful retirement benefits.

○ *Part IV: Caveat Emptor* outlines the importance of legal, ethical, and defensible advanced planning strategies and provides a blueprint for selecting and working with high-quality specialists.

○ *Part V: Being Wealthy* introduces some core concepts for managing and deploying your future fortune in ways that align with your personal priorities, needs, and objectives.

Most books are a highly collaborative effort and this one is no different. Our co-authors Carlo Scissura and Frank Seneco added dimensions to business ownership and advanced planning we could not have achieved without their input. And we are grateful to the partners of accounting firm O'Connor Davies for helping us understand the technical challenges facing businesses and their owners and build case studies that reflect optimal solutions to actual situations.

As a business owner there is much to be learned from this treatise on advanced planning, but we believe the most important takeaway is that you can (and should) fortify your life's work. There are actions you can take on your own and strategies you can pursue in partnership with select professionals who will enable you to **structure, protect, and transfer your assets in the most strategic and legally tax-efficient manner.**

With *Maximizing Personal Wealth,* we hope to begin a new cycle of informed empowerment that will balance, and eventually eliminate, the cycle of wealth destruction we've witnessed for so long.

Russ Alan Prince and **Hannah Shaw Grove**
New York, NY
December 2014

PART I

CREATING PERSONAL WEALTH

FOR MANY, THE GREATEST ADVANTAGE OF BEING
WEALTHY IS ALL ABOUT HAVING MORE OPTIONS.
It's all about moving from necessities to preferences. It's about
accommodating wants as opposed to stressing over needs.
As such, it's a given that a great many people are exceedingly
interested in being rich. However, becoming affluent is not
all that common—to say the least. It requires doing the
right things and doing them well.

Owning a business is usually one of those right things.
Unfortunately, owning a business is commonly insufficient.
There are ways of looking at situations and actions that will
significantly increase the likelihood you'll become wealthy.
We refer to this mind-set and supporting behaviors as
Millionaire Intelligence.

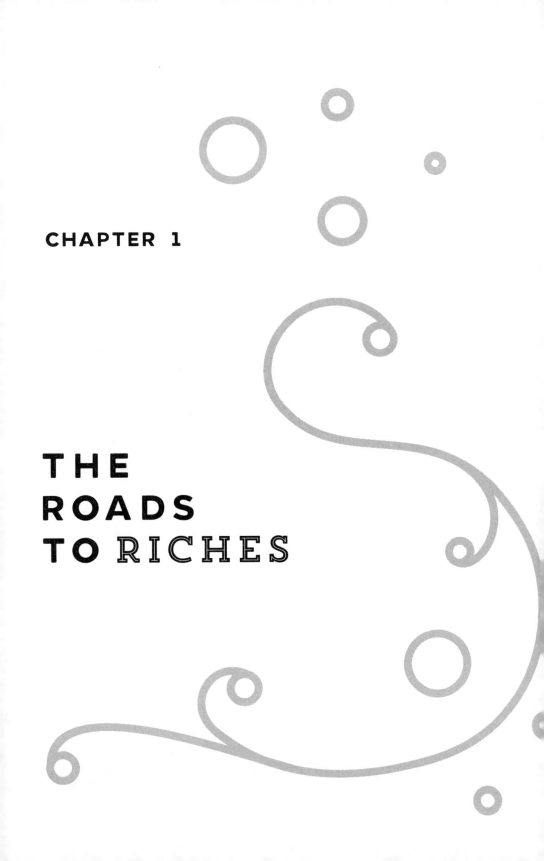

CHAPTER 1

THE
ROADS
TO RICHES

There are many ways—both legal and illegal—to become wealthy. That being said, what's clear and repeatedly proven out in the research is that business ownership is the most powerful and consistent way to become wealthy... potentially extremely wealthy. However, there are other ways to become rich such as marrying for money.

MARRYING FOR MONEY

Perhaps the most fascinating way to get rich is through marriage. And while there are many high-profile and successful examples of this strategy regularly on display in the tabloids, our research shows that most people approach the opportunity with a highly personalized point-of-view that translates into under-sized goals and disappointing results.

In a survey, we spoke with almost 1,000 unmarried people with average annual incomes ranging from $30,000 to $60,000 (Exhibit 1.1). The majority of people recognize that money can ease a lot of concerns and "marrying up" makes perfect sense provided the circumstances are acceptable.

EXHIBIT 1.1:
Unmarried Individuals
% N = 956 INDIVIDUALS

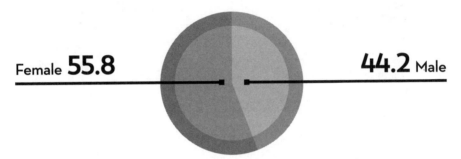

Female **55.8**   **44.2** Male

About two-thirds of our survey respondents expressed a high degree of interest in marrying someone for his or her money and the associated fiscal security if that person was "likable" and "not ugly" (Exhibit 1.2). Proportionately, more women than men reported being amenable to the idea, though one female respondent explained the inverse relationship between looks and wealth by stating "the uglier he is, the more money he has to have."

EXHIBIT 1.2:
"Very" or "Extremely" Willing to Marry for Money
% N = 956 INDIVIDUALS

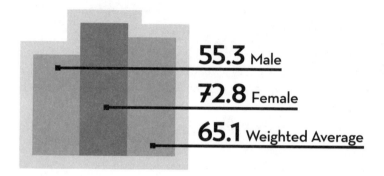

55.3 Male

72.8 Female

65.1 Weighted Average

It turns out that $1 million is a magic number for many. When queried about the amount of money it would take to seal the deal, every respondent gave a figure that exceeded $1 million—in some cases, however, not by much. Men said it would take an average $1.1 million to consider marrying someone they didn't love, while women set their sights nearly four times higher at $3.8 million to take the plunge (Exhibit 1.3).

EXHIBIT 1.3
Amount of Money Required (in $ millions)
N = 956 INDIVIDUALS

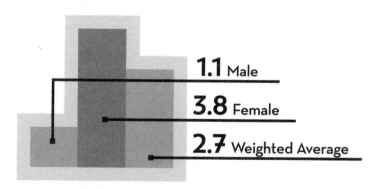

1.1 Male

3.8 Female

2.7 Weighted Average

While it's certainly possible to become wealthy, there tend to be all sorts of complications from the quality of the relationship to who might be in charge. More than ever, marrying for money proves somewhat limited if the relationship collapses. From prenuptial agreements to the deft use of trusts, if the relationship fails, the money evaporates. Also, we've been informed by people who've gone this route that it's hard work—an awful lot of hard work.

SIX PRINCIPAL KINDS OF
PERSONAL WEALTH

EQUITY WEALTH

Throughout the world, equity wealth is the most common route to affluence. This is wealth created by having an equity stake in a prosperous revenue generating entity, which is usually an ongoing successful enterprise.

POST-EQUITY WEALTH

This kind of wealth is created when the owner of the "enterprise" sells his or her stake to another person or company and subsequently gets rich (or richer). Equity stakes are often illiquid assets; so many people only realize many of the benefits of personal wealth once the sale is complete.

CORPORATE WEALTH

Senior officers in public and private corporations have amassed sizable estates from handsome compensation packages including bonuses, deferred compensation, restricted stock, and stock options.

INHERITED WEALTH

"Trust babies" of all ages are the beneficiaries of someone else's success. While captivating and sometimes attention grabbing, they're comparatively rare. In fact, inherited wealth represents less than ten percent of all private wealth.

ILLEGAL WEALTH

Either in the form of criminal activities or flight capital, illegal wealth is extensive and extreme. It's worth noting, however, that the wealth of most successful criminals is derived from their "equity ownership" of an illicit enterprise.

FORTUITOUS WEALTH

The least likely and least predictable way of getting rich is by getting lucky; say by winning the lottery or finding an abandoned Van Gogh painting at the side of the road.

While there are various ways to become wealthy, having a stake in a successful enterprise is the most likely way to do so. Either the business is successful enough to make you affluent (i.e., equity wealth), or by selling the business you become wealthy or wealthier (i.e., post-equity wealth).

In researching the exceptionally wealthy, we consistently found that having a piece of the action—predominantly an equity stake in a company—was the way most people amassed their fortunes. In a survey of 661 private jet owners (individuals with an average net worth of $89 million and an average annual income of $9 million), about three-quarters of them derived their wealth from equity or post-equity ownership stakes. In another survey of 376 single-family offices, the underlying source of wealth was overwhelmingly equity or post-equity wealth. Approximately nine out of every ten family fortunes is directly tied to having equity in a successful enterprise.

What's evident is that owning a business—provided the business does well—is the most likely route to becoming a millionaire or a millionaire many times over. While there are many reasons for owning a business, personal wealth creation is certainly high on the list.

MORE MONEY

In our survey of 513 business owners (see *Appendix A: Survey of Business Owners*), we found that a little more than nine out of ten of them want to become significantly wealthier than they are today (Exhibit 1.4). Moreover, all of them strongly recognize their ability to become wealthier is a function of the success of their business.

EXHIBIT 1.4:

Want to Become Significantly Wealthier
% N = 513 BUSINESS OWNERS

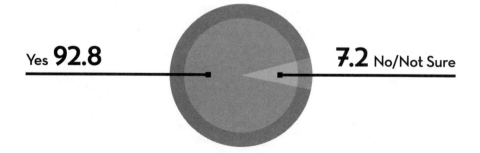

Yes **92.8**   **7.2** No/Not Sure

There are often many reasons business owners want to be wealthier. Taking care of loved one regularly tops the list (Exhibit 1.5). The success of the business and their ability to maximize personal wealth is usually instrumental in this regard.

EXHIBIT 1.5:
Make Sure Loved Ones are Financially Taken Care Of
% N = 513 BUSINESS OWNERS

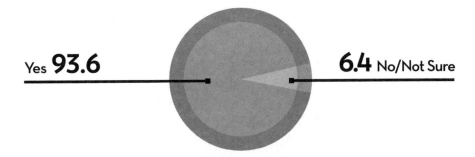

Yes **93.6**   **6.4** No/Not Sure

At the same time, about seven out of ten business owners said they're interested in doing more to support worthy charitable causes (Exhibit 1.6). Again, the success of their business and their ability to translate that success into personal wealth can be significant in enabling these business owners to be more philanthropic.

EXHIBIT 1.6:
Interested in Doing More to Support Worthy Charitable Causes
% N = 513 BUSINESS OWNERS

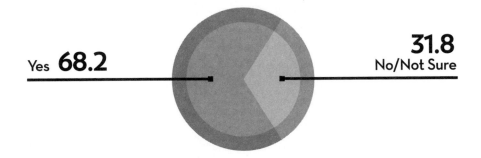

Yes **68.2**   **31.8** No/Not Sure

Whatever the constellation of motivations, the ability to become increasingly affluent is, in many ways, a cornerstone for many business owners. While business success is the primary generator of personal wealth, the ability to mitigate taxes in addition to derailing frivolous lawsuits can prove critical to the amount of personal wealth you're able to accumulate. To this end, we have advanced planning (see *Part II: Advanced Planning*).

CONCLUSION

What's clear is that the route to personal wealth—especially when it comes to the creation of larger fortunes—is by having equity in a successful enterprise. While having an equity position that translates into substantial monies is generally critical, it takes a *very special person* to make it all happen and to become wealthy. In fact, we've repeatedly discerned that self-made millionaires think and, more importantly, act differently than those who are less affluent, and this mind-set and the associated patterns of behavior are generally more pronounced as the level of wealth increases.

We refer to these characteristics that dramatically increase a person's ability to join the ranks of the self-made millionaires (and, potentially, though it's quite a long shot, become a self-made billionaire) as *Millionaire Intelligence*. In the next chapter we'll explore some of the key concepts of *Millionaire Intelligence* that result in significant personal wealth creation.

CHAPTER 2

MILLIONAIRE INTELLIGENCE

BY
RUSS ALAN PRINCE AND
HANNAH SHAW GROVE

The big picture is that having an equity stake in a business is clearly the predominant way to become wealthy. However, your ability to capitalize on business opportunities and related situations is essential to becoming wealthy.

Millionaire Intelligence is the framework many business owners have employed to join the ranks of self-made millionaires. *Millionaire Intelligence* is based on more than a quarter century of empirical investigations comparing the business-building and personal wealth-creating thought processes and behaviors of self-made millionaires with those of the rest of the population. Along the same lines, the research illustrates the differences among various cohorts of self-made successes, from millionaires all the way up the line to the super-rich (net worth = $500 million or more).

The results of this research show there are very pronounced and distinct ways of thinking and approaching wealth creation that change in both intensity and nature as net worth increases. For example, there are decisive actions separating self-made millionaires from wannabes. We've been able to determine the often highly nuanced behaviors, which distinguish those lower on the private wealth hierarchy from those at the very top. The result of this extensive program of research is *Millionaire Intelligence*.

SELECT COMPONENTS OF MILLIONAIRE INTELLIGENCE

For illustrative purposes, the *Millionaire Intelligence* framework can be divided into two sets of factors (Exhibit 2.1). One set of factors is the way you think about the business world and how you approach doing business. It's about how to work most effectively with associates, competitors, and everyone else. By and large, this is the mind-set of self-made millionaires. We've identified the insights and acumen that produce this mind-set. Without the right *mind-set*, you're not going to effectively navigate to the outcomes which produce a noteworthy personal fortune.

The other set of factors is the actions—the behaviors—that are key to driving business success. First you must understand which actions are most likely to produce the desired outcomes. But ultimately, it's the mind-set that drives the commitment to taking the requisite actions.

EXHIBIT 2.1:
Millionaire Intelligence

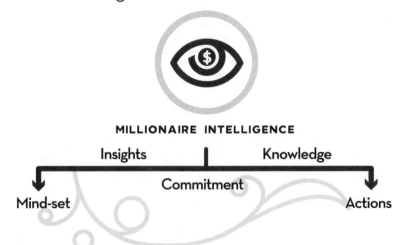

MILLIONAIRE INTELLIGENCE

Insights | Knowledge

Commitment

Mind-set | Actions

While *Millionaire Intelligence* has many interconnected synergistic components, the intent here is to highlight just a few of them. Moreover, in *Chapter 3: Bargaining Brilliance*, we discuss how many self-made millionaires negotiate as this is a skill set that's consistently shown to be instrumental to their success. Let's begin with:

○ **Committing to creating personal wealth**

○ **Putting yourself in the line of money**

○ **Using failure to refine and focus**

Committing to creating personal wealth. Truth be told, many people would like to be rich but haven't devoted the time or effort necessary to get there. Doing so can often mean being faced with choices that help you reach your goal of being wealthy at the expense of something else that may be important to you. This means having a clear sense that amassing money is one of a number of very important objectives and, by doing so, you consciously prioritize activities with the highest potential return which may necessitate assigning a lower priority to many other things in your life.

A commitment to creating personal wealth is regularly a core driver of success for self-made millionaires. To operationalize your commitment, you need to specify how much is enough. This is your financial end-goal. A few aspects of financial end-goal setting include:

○ **You need to avoid "shiny objects" that appear promising but only distract you from your financial end-goal.**

○ **Along the way to your financial end-goal, you need to determine meaningful milestones.**

○ **As you get closer to reaching your financial end-goal, there's more than a good chance you're going to re-set it higher.**

While it's certainly possible to become personally wealthy without it being an express goal, it's much less likely to happen. By wanting money and understanding why, you're much more inclined to be financially successful.

Putting yourself in the line of money. Simply put, some endeavors are more fruitful and rewarding than others. For instance, building a successful business is habitually more lucrative than being a social worker employed by the city. Along the same lines, being your own boss usually gives you a greater chance for personal wealth than working for somebody else.

Since most skills are portable, it only makes sense that self-made millionaires apply theirs in the situations offering the highest paybacks. Following this perspective means you pursue fields and initiatives that have the highest potential for outsize returns now and in the future and often includes owning your own business.

As we saw in the previous chapter, having equity in a business, one that you're striving to make exceptionally successful, is probably the very best way to put yourself in the line of money. At the same time, what's very characteristic of self-made millionaires is that they "run the numbers." Based on meticulous calculations or an instinctive familiarity with the financials, they look at each initiative and derive projected returns. The following are three guidelines for running the numbers:

○ It's easy to do, but you must avoid falling in love with an initiative.

○ You must always work and re-work the assumptions.

○ It's essential to be able to justify your assessments under various scenarios.

By being a business owner, you're clearly putting yourself in the line of money. Still, you need to look at each business decision as a way to ensure you stay firmly in the line of money, which generally requires running the numbers.

Using failure to improve and refocus. Failure is inevitable, so most self-made millionaires don't worry about avoiding it. Instead, they focus on learning from each experience and using the lessons to get an advantage the next time around.

Rather than obsessing about lost opportunities and getting discouraged, you should study your failures and do all you can to prevent repeating missteps. Central to "using" failure is perseverance. When confronted by professional setbacks, self-made millionaires are often energized. The following are some aspects of the way you can make failure an ally:

○ **You need to autopsy your failures, meaning evaluating what went wrong and why.**

○ **You must be brutally honest with yourself when evaluating the mistakes that were made.**

○ **You must work diligently not to repeat the same mistakes.**

What really matters is how you handle failure. You need to make your failures work for you, and by critically dissecting them, you're able to learn somber lessons that you must take to heart.

CONNECT FOR PROFIT AND RESULTS

Networking is generally recognized as an essential and often optimal means for personal and professional success. Even so, it's painfully clear that most people are NOT capable and prosperous networkers.

Most individuals, including many business owners, approach networking as a near-random exercise. They talk to other people, some of whom might even prove useful. Their intent is muddled and their focus is blurry. For the most part, the majority of people seeking to gain advantages by networking are badly mistaking activity for productivity, incorrectly crediting the smallest of advances as being monumental.

Self-made millionaires regularly think about networking as a means to an end—finding the person, the information, or the resources that gets them one step closer to their personal and professional milestones, which, in turn, gets them closer to their financial end-goal.

While it's important to have many valuable contacts, you also probably need to maintain a small but deep network of relationships leading not to friendship, but to personal wealth and influence. This form of nodal networking maximizes the time and effort spent toward realizing profit and identifying those things that can further enhance your wealth. A few core aspects of nodal networking include:

○ **You must learn who the contacts of your contacts are so as to potentially benefit from the people they know well.**

○ **You must build "bench strength"—identifying people who can replace members of your nodal network when appropriate.**

○ **You must internalize the concept and behavior called N.E.X.T.— Never Extend eXtra Time—so as not to waste resources on unproductive relationships.**

Effective networking like negotiation (see *Chapter 3: Bargaining Brilliance*) is regularly essential to pecuniary achievements. Being strategic and focused when it comes to networking is vital. In this regard, there are four questions you should be asking yourself when networking:

WHAT are you seeking to accomplish? Goals are essential, especially when it comes to networking. By adroitly setting goals for each relationship and even each interaction, you'll be able to focus and improve your efforts. By being quite clear about your agenda, you'll also quickly know when it's time to disengage and when it's worthwhile to persevere.

WHO can help you achieve your goals? Knowing what you want to accomplish, you'll be better able to triage the many people you meet so as to determine which relationships can be most productive. At the same time, you're able to proactively identify those people who can prove valuable enabling you to constructively reach out to them.

WHY do they care? Knowing what you want and even knowing who to talk to is the easy part. Generally, self-made millionaires work with the concept of "enlightened self-interest." Thus, they're exceedingly determined to identify the core motivations, dominant preferences, and critical concerns of the people who can help them so that information can be leveraged into mutually rewarding action.

HOW are you going to get them to care about you achieving your goals? Knowing why other people care and being able to connect these reasons to your agenda can create a powerful results-orientated network. Self-made millionaires tend to be very good at creating alignment between their goals and what will make other people care about them achieving their goals.

Being able to effectively answer these questions can be transformational. While the answers will many times change due to fluctuating circumstances, the value of thinking strategically and purposefully—like the majority of self-made millionaires—will likely make monumental differences in enabling you to get substantial results when networking.

Millionaire Intelligence is quite learnable. This has resulted in our ability to provide Personal Wealth Creation Programs.

PERSONAL WEALTH CREATION PROGRAMS

As noted, our clinical interest in the genesis of meaningful, if not extreme, personal wealth is many decades old. Presently, the insights and methodologies predicated on that interest form the foundation of a fascinating and profitable boutique consulting practice, the development of Personal Wealth Creation Programs. There are three scenarios for these programs:

Extensions. How much is enough? For some people, the sky's not the limit. We're periodically engaged by the wealthy who desire to be meaningfully wealthier.

Example: A business owner is worth close to $200 million after selling a company she helped to found. She knows she mishandled the transaction with her partners as well as with the buyer, costing her a great deal. Now, she wants to triple her net worth by financing new firms, but this time her interest is squarely on how she'll benefit including how to capitalize on her extensive network of contacts.

Turnarounds. There are people who were once extremely wealthy—but for various reasons—lost a substantial portion, if not all, of their fortunes. Now, they want to regain their wealth.

Example: A musician/entrepreneur/business owner let the high-living celebrity lifestyle distract him to the tune of a $50 million loss while racking up debts twice as high. First, it's necessary to restructure his debt and control expenses. Then the aim is to take a very proactive approach to rebuilding his business and reputation in a very different musical and media environment than when he created his fortune.

Lift-offs. Business owners who want to create substantial wealth but have in some way hit a glass ceiling. These individuals want to fast-track to serious personal wealth and need some guidance and support.

Example: A successful business owner worth a few million dollars desires to cultivate a "great fortune" so he can underwrite pancreatic cancer research in honor of his deceased son. His altruistic nature is working against him in dramatic ways. A pressing example is the way he tends to negotiate instead of the way he needs to (see *Chapter 3: Bargaining Brilliance*).

A PERSONAL NOTE

While we have a proven track record of getting results—of assisting business owners in amassing significant personal wealth—a not insubstantial part of our success is due to the fact we're highly selective in whom we take on as a client. It's akin to the top universities. By admitting only some of the finest students there are, it shouldn't be a surprise that many of these students go on to have great careers.

The best candidates for Personal Wealth Creation Programs have five core characteristics:

○ **A strong desire to become wealthy.**

○ **The mind-set, talents, and skills that can be refined and directed on what it's going to take to extend, fast track, or rebuild a personal fortune.**

○ **A high-quality professional and/or personal network that can be readily and adroitly enhanced and monetized.**

○ **Financial or other resources (e.g., brand, intellectual capital, etc.) that can be innovatively leveraged.**

○ **A willingness to listen and try.**

What has proven fascinating is that except for the first and last of the five characteristics (i.e., desire to become wealthy and a willingness to listen and try), most of our clients didn't realize the extent to which they already possess the other three. Many business owners do indeed have these other three characteristics, and it often takes a little probing to confirm that they do.

While there are never any guarantees, business owners with these characteristics have enormous potential to take *Millionaire Intelligence* and amass significant personal fortunes.

CONCLUSION

Let's be totally transparent. There is no secret knowledge. There are no magic runes, no alchemic formulas, and no transformational rituals that result in creating a personal fortune. Being one with the universe, thinking positive, speaking victories, visualizing the preferred state, studying the ancient grimoires (and we have an extensive collection of such arcane tomes) will not make someone wealthy.

With respect to *Millionaire Intelligence*, all we've done is apply academic rigor to identify the mind-set and behavioral patterns that produce significant wealth by studying those who did it—self-made millionaires. If we can be credited with anything, we've systematized these perspectives and developed effective pedagogical methodologies for mastering them. We can also be credited with being able to work closely with business owners to keep the process of creating considerable personal wealth tightly "on track."

Very often, critical to becoming wealthy is the ability to skillfully negotiate. In the context of *Millionaire Intelligence,* we refer to this as *bargaining brilliance:* the topic of the next chapter.

CHAPTER 3

BARGAINING BRILLIANCE

BY
RUSS ALAN PRINCE AND
FRANK V. CARONE

 critical skill set to becoming a very successful business owner and, consequently, personally wealthy is an ability to adroitly negotiate.

In many scenarios, the more proficient you are at bargaining, the more likely your business will thrive. Furthermore, being a skilled negotiator will enable you to achieve greater success in a variety of professional platforms along with personal arenas.

BUSINESS OWNERS WANT TO BE BETTER NEGOTIATORS

About nine out of ten of the business owners we surveyed considered themselves good negotiators, with 20 percent of them saying they're very or extremely good negotiators (Exhibit 3.1).

EXHIBIT 3.1:
Negotiating Ability
% N = 513 BUSINESS OWNERS

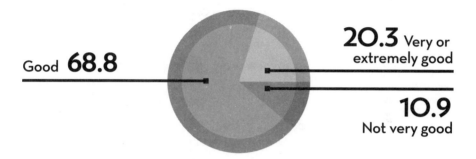

Good **68.8**

20.3 Very or extremely good

10.9 Not very good

What's more insightful is that a little more than three-quarters of them say they're interested in becoming more proficient negotiators (Exhibit 3.2). Although many of these business owners consider themselves capable or more than capable, they understand that becoming a better negotiator has multiplicative positive effects. These business owners realize even getting just a little bit better can make a profound difference.

EXHIBIT 3.2:
Desire to Become More Proficient Negotiators
% N = 513 BUSINESS OWNERS

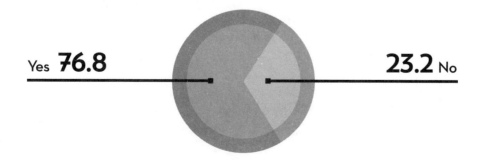

Yes **76.8**

23.2 No

In constructing the operational methodologies predicated on *Millionaire Intelligence,* we've been able to develop a highly systematic approach to negotiation we refer to as *bargaining brilliance.* While this approach is exceptionally effective due to its foundational elements, we recognize it doesn't philosophically appeal to everyone.

Let's begin with the conceptual and philosophical underpinnings of the methodology.

"I WIN, YOU WHATEVER"

The "I win, you whatever" philosophy in the center of bargaining brilliance doesn't mean that in a negotiation you must be a winner *and* the person across the table from you must be a loser. The two of you can certainly conclude the negotiations as winners, which is the optimal scenario. However, the "I win, you whatever" philosophy says that it's essential for your success to walk away from an important negotiation as a winner, irrespective of the ability of the other party to reach his or her goals. Simply put: "You win!"

Self-made millionaires realize that the only way they're going to win when negotiating is by carefully and forcefully looking out for their own interests. This is not about being selfish or egotistical; it's about being realistic. It's about being pragmatic. It's the way to succeed.

While advocates of the win-win philosophy frequently talk about long-term relationships and fairness for all, according to most self-made millionaires, if you're not looking out for yourself, it's highly unlikely anyone with whom you're negotiating will be looking out for you either. To see the potential alternatives, consider the matrix in Exhibit 3.3.

EXHIBIT 3.3:
Negotiating Results Matrix
SOURCE: I WIN, YOU WHATEVER (2013)

		YOU	
		LOSE	WIN
COUNTER PARTY	WIN	Substandard	Optimal
	LOSE	Substandard	Excellent

As noted, the optimal scenario is one where all parties conclude the negotiations as winners. And, we strongly recommend you strive for this outcome. It is the best result and can have the greatest long-term benefits. However, if everyone cannot be successful, as long as you achieve your goals, then the negotiations are still a success. If you lose, whether the other party wins or loses, for you the result of the negotiation was substandard.

This philosophy is at the core of the way a great many self-made millionaires bargain, and it's a substantial part of the reason they're repeatedly so effective. It's central to their ability to amass considerable personal wealth. While they usually have no problem with seeing the other party doing well, they themselves must win.

Strategically, the way to be a winner when negotiating is encapsulated in the performance equation.

THE PERFORMANCE EQUATION

Self-made millionaires usually approach business negotiations in profoundly different ways than less financially successful individuals. Whether establishing joint ventures, creating strategic alliances, bargaining with clients and suppliers, or selling and buying companies, not only are they exceedingly focused and disciplined, but they also employ an array of stratagems and tactics likely to radically increase their ability to achieve the outcomes they desire. They're quite effective at getting the terms they want and structuring the deal for their benefit.

As noted, through in-depth research of these self-made millionaires, we identified the various components of highly successful negotiating, and at its core is the performance equation:

PERFORMANCE=

PERSPECTIVE + **PURPOSE** + **PREPARATION** + **PROCESS**

Let's briefly examine each of the variables in this performance equation.

PERSPECTIVE is a self-made millionaire's cognitive bargaining orientation. These business owners intensely focus on achieving their agendas, often maintaining a single mindedness toward their critical business goals to which all else outside of this is noise. The following are select key concepts:

○ **Everyone—yes, everyone—is dysfunctional.** Your intent is to gain an advantage by understanding, and thereby owning, the other party's issues while avoiding the exploitation of your weaknesses by the counter party.

○ **Success breeds "enemies."** This is a structural phenomenon resulting in some of the best negotiators often being vilified. As such, antagonistic feelings from the others are inevitable, and it's important to not let the possibility of becoming denigrated be an impediment to achieving significant results.

PURPOSE is what self-made millionaires want out of their negotiation. It's the outcomes they seek. These business owners are very good at defining their range of negotiating goals and maintaining their focus on the high-end of these ranges. Moreover, they're proficient at connecting their negotiating goals to their overall business goals and related objectives. The following are select key concepts:

○ **Your negotiating goals need to be slightly unreasonable.** Negotiating goals are very likely to prove motivating and attainable when they make enough sense to the opponent, but still make that person effectively uneasy. This requires you to have a thorough understanding of the rationale— on all sides—for the goals.

○ **Sticking to your high-end goals is essential.** Unfortunately, many business owners end up with bad deals by surrendering on critical terms. This not only results in remorse, but it can also contribute to subsequent actions that derail future opportunities. You must understand that no deal is infinitely better than a bad deal, and you need to define a "bad deal" in advance of a negotiation.

PREPARATION is the homework self-made millionaires conduct before facing off with the people with whom they're negotiating. It's how you evaluate the character of the negotiations, the overall strategic approach you choose to take, the formulation of key arguments, and how you derive—or intend to derive—advantages. To obtain the best results, self-made millionaires prepare intensely, if not passionately; they have a plan and so should you. The following are select key concepts:

- **You need to negotiate the people.** While understanding the terms of a deal is very important, success will more likely come from understanding the people sitting across the table from you. Being attuned to their dysfunction (see above), their need for the deal, their alternatives, and other relevant issues and critical concerns can be greatly empowering.

- **You must honestly evaluate the situation.** A candid assessment of your relative position vis-a-vis the counter party will dictate the most appropriate bargaining strategies to employ. Depending on the respective advantages each side has, the need to be clever can become integral.

PROCESS is the give and take between parties in the negotiation. It's how you make your case based on the previous stage tempered by the way the interaction is progressing. What's habitually central to being effective at this time is the nature and quality of the relationship between you and those sitting across from you. The following are select key concepts:

- **Active listening is a cornerstone skill.** Self-made millionaires truly capture and understand the messages other people are sending. It includes assessing both nonverbal and verbal messages. As an active listener, you understand the context of the negotiations—the current situation, the person, and scenario's back-story, coupled with the other party's expectations.

- **A tremendous advantage is gained by making anger work for you.** By not letting anger get in the way, you can avoid magnifying insecurities, which can produce more anger, cloud reason, and result in poor decision making. Meanwhile, you need to capitalize on the situation when the party with whom you're negotiating gets angry.

There are many concepts and tactics that derive from and interrelate to the performance equation. When the components of the equation have been handled adeptly, it increases your chances for a promising outcome. Your ability to think strategically is the driver of the methodology.

CONCLUSION

Bargaining brilliance with the "I win, you whatever" philosophy at its core embodies the negotiating thinking and practices of a great many self-made millionaires. What's evident as seen in the research results as well as in working with the business owners is that many of them are quite capable negotiators, yet are interested in stepping-up their expertise.

Bargaining brilliance like all of *Millionaire Intelligence* is very learnable. There aren't any secrets to negotiating at this level of proficiency, as the knowledge is easily accessible. Negotiating success, therefore, is much more a matter of doing than knowing.

While it's useful to understand how combining equity with *Millionaire Intelligence* can produce considerable personal wealth, our focus now shifts to ways you can maximize your personal wealth through advanced planning.

Frank V. Carone is a Partner at Abrams, Fensterman, Fensterman, Eisman, Formato, Ferrara & Wolf, LLP (www.abramslaw.com). Frank has extensive experience in many complex areas of the law including Criminal Defense, Regulatory Compliance, Banking, Litigation and Corporate Governance. Mr. Carone is regularly consulted by attorneys and members of the profession on mortgage compliance, litigation, corporate governance, and complex criminal matters.

PART II

ADVANCED
PLANING

HAVING CREATED SOME LEVEL OF PERSONAL WEALTH, business owners confront the situation of preserving their hard-earned affluence in the face of those who are oh-so eager to share it with them such as tax authorities and predacious litigants. Maximizing personal wealth is ofttimes about making certain you maintain the monies for which you labored so intensely.

With the absolute requirements of adhering to lawful and, more importantly, the highest ethical standards, there are often a multitude of financial and legal strategies that you can employ. Some of these strategies are also effective in enabling you to enhance your personal wealth because they negate the financially corrosive effect of taxes. All in all, these strategies generically fall under the heading of advanced planning.

CHAPTER 4

DEFINING
ADVANCED
PLANNING

usiness ownership is likely the best way to become wealthy (see *Chapter 1: The Roads to Riches*). However, wealth can be fleeting. Research with the wealthy, with the exceptionally wealthy, and with the super-rich consistently identifies a prominent and often persistent concern: *financial fragility*. This is the recognition that wealth, even great wealth—Croesus fortunes—can dissolve or be eradicated. It can be vaporized by hubris, financial mismanagement often due to entrusting monies to incompetents, and, too commonly, stolen by financial predators.

By and large, it takes so much time and effort to create significant personal wealth that losing it rarely provides the wealth creator—the business owner—the opportunity to do it again. Moreover, being wealthy and then losing a fortune can easily have serious adverse psychological consequences. Severe anxiety and depression often top a very long list of emotional maladies.

ADVANCED PLANNING

Put simply, ensuring the continuity of meaningful personal wealth is more than being able to amass significant monies; it's also the ability to maintain such fortunes. Thus, there's often the need for advanced planning.

Advanced planning is the skillful leveraging of legal, regulatory, and financial expertise to enhance and safeguard an individual's or a family's net worth.

The objectives and benefits of advanced planning are hard to dispute. Without question, there are many ways for you to legitimately capitalize on the tax code and legal system to protect and sometimes enhance your wealth. At the same time, there are people and organizations such as tax authorities and litigants who want to share your wealth even though you would prefer otherwise.

Every government wants its cut, and advanced planning strategies can help lawfully minimize tax obligations. In an increasingly litigious society, business owners in addition to their businesses are prime targets for unfounded, many times silly and malicious lawsuits. Advanced planning offers an effective way to structure assets to discourage lawsuits and provide legal shelter from potential plaintiffs.

Operationally speaking, advanced planning results in the repositioning and restructuring of assets to preserve and sometimes increase the wealth of business owners. Advanced planning entails leveraging the legal, tax, and regulatory systems to provide one or more of the following three often interconnected services (Exhibit 4.1):

○ Wealth enhancement

○ Estate planning

○ Asset protection planning

EXHIBIT 4.1:
The Three Interconnected Services of Advanced Planning

Wealth Enhancement • Estate Planning • Asset Protection

These three sets of services interlock thematically and are important to varying degrees depending on your specific situation. Let's now consider each one.

Wealth Enhancement

There are situations when you can make your money work harder for you by lessening or eliminating taxes.

Are you aware of these situations and have you taken the best advantage of these opportunities?

Making your money work harder for you translates into more of it. And there are ways to heighten and sometimes even super-charge your ability to boost the wealth you've created with your business.

Wealth enhancement is the process of using advanced planning strategies to mitigate taxes resulting in greater personal wealth creation.

With respect to investment management, for example, your goal is to produce the best possible performance. The key is to determine the current timing, character, and amount of taxable income. When it comes to investment income, the ideal transition is from income to short-term capital gains, to long-term capital gains, to tax deferral, and ultimately to no taxes whatsoever. This continuum drives the opportunities and the deliverables of the advanced planner with the goal of moving your situation as far along this continuum as is practicable under the given circumstances.

There are a wide variety of strategies that can be utilized to enhance wealth (see *Chapter 8: Solving Problems*). The adept use of charitable trusts, for example, can be instrumental in enhancing wealth while also enabling business owners to appreciably benefit others. For wealthy business owners with significant liquid assets, some of the most attractive strategies incorporate private placement life insurance.

The use of qualified retirement plans and other retirement-oriented strategies is another way for you to enhance your personal wealth (see *Chapter 9: Retirement Solutions*). This is a function of both the tax deductions and the tax-free growth of assets funding the plans. The key is choosing retirement solutions based on your strategic and financial objectives.

Research findings. Not surprisingly, nearly all the business owners surveyed are extremely or very interested in ways to legally lower their personal tax bills (Exhibit 4.2). Among those who are interested, only about a quarter of them are actively working with professionals to do so (Exhibit 4.3).

EXHIBIT 4.2:
Interested in Ways to Lower Personal Taxes
% N = 513 BUSINESS OWNERS

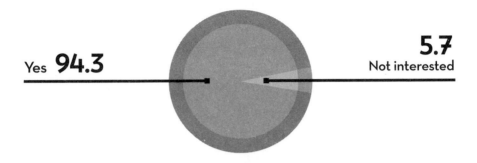

Yes **94.3**

5.7
Not interested

EXHIBIT 4.3:
Working with Professionals to Lower Personal Taxes
% N = 484 BUSINESS OWNERS

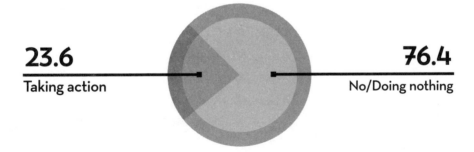

23.6
Taking action

76.4
No/Doing nothing

Although there's a strong interest among business owners in enhancing their wealth by lawfully lowering their tax bill, relatively few of them are actively pursuing the range of opportunities. While many are doing something such as establishing a qualified retirement plan, for example, few business owners are actively evaluating and implementing qualified retirement plans that maximize their own personal wealth (see *Chapter 9: Retirement Solutions*).

Estate Planning

 Death—hopefully a long way off—is nevertheless an eventuality. Have you prepared financially as best you can for this inevitability?

As long as there are estate taxes, as long as there are intergenerational consid-erations, as long as there are interconnected business interests, and as long as immortality is only a dream, there will be a need for estate planning. Business owners are looking to achieve a certain agenda and to do so in as tax-efficient a manner as possible. However, when it comes to estate planning, it's important to keep in mind that taxes are not the tail that should wag the dog.

Estate planning is the process of legally structuring the future disposition of current and projected assets.

Basic estate planning employing such strategies and financial products as credit-shelter trusts and traditional life insurance is fairly straightforward and sufficient for many business owners. If your financial picture and goals are more compli-cated, there are a plethora of more sophisticated strategies (see *Chapter 8: Solving Problems*) including self-canceling installment notes, grantor retained annuity trusts, and remainder purchase marital trusts.

You might be seriously committed to various charitable causes. The ability to now and in the future provide significant monies and resources to worthy philanthropic organizations is possible through adept estate planning.

Research findings. A little more than seven out of ten business owners have an estate plan which is defined as having, at a minimum, a will (Exhibit 4.4). Among the 138 business owners without an estate plan, half of them have not done the planning because the topic is very hard to deal with (Exhibit 4.5). From facing the prospect of death to needing to make difficult decisions concerning the disposition of assets including the future fate of the business, estate planning can very well be arduous and emotionally nerve-wracking.

About 30 percent said they didn't have an estate plan because there wasn't a need. Although there might not be estate tax concerns, it's usually advisable that everyone have an estate plan, even if it's only a will. This is especially the case for business owners as the company is an asset and part of the estate. The remaining business owners without estate plans cited a lack of time and the expense as the primary reasons for not having one.

EXHIBIT 4.4:
Have an Estate Plan
% N = 513 BUSINESS OWNERS

Yes **73.1**　　　　　　　　　　　　**26.9** No

EXHIBIT 4.5:
Why No Estate Plan
% N = 138 BUSINESS OWNERS

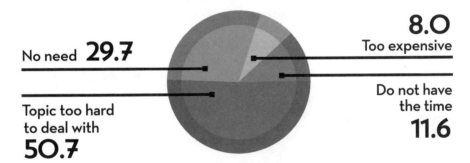

No need **29.7**

Topic too hard
to deal with
50.7

8.0
Too expensive

Do not have
the time
11.6

For those business owners with an estate plan, most of them are more than five years old (Exhibit 4.6). Almost a quarter of the estate plans are two to five years old, with the remaining 12 percent less than two years old. Because of continual changes in the tax laws, estate plans that are more than a few years old are likely to be out-of-date and fail to take maximum advantage of available tax-saving opportunities.

EXHIBIT 4.6:
Age of Estate Plan
% N = 375 BUSINESS OWNERS

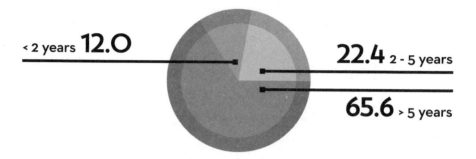

< 2 years **12.0**

22.4 2 - 5 years

65.6 > 5 years

What's even more telling is that more than half of these business owners report that they're wealthier since they created their estate plans (Exhibit 4.7). More importantly, nearly seven out of ten reported that since they created their estate plans, they've experienced life changing events (Exhibit 4.8). These events can be anything from divorce to the birth of children or grandchildren to the death of prospective guardians, and so forth.

EXHIBIT 4.7:
Wealthier Since the Estate Plan
% N = 375 BUSINESS OWNERS

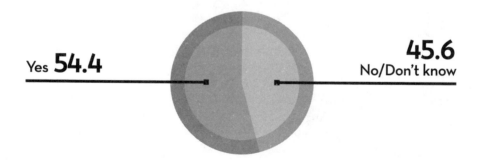

Yes **54.4**

45.6
No/Don't know

EXHIBIT 4.8:
Experienced a Life Changing Event since the Estate Plan
% N = 375 BUSINESS OWNERS

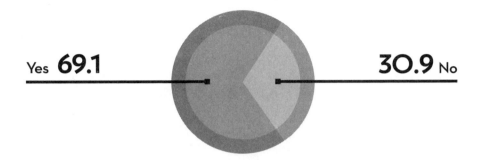

Yes **69.1**   **30.9** No

What this tells us is that from changes in the tax laws to changes in the lives and wealth of the business owners, for a sizable number of them, their estate plans are likely outdated. In order to attain the greatest benefits from estate planning, you need to stay on top of the matter and revise your estate plans when appropriate.

Asset Protection Planning

Undeserved and frivolous lawsuits are often a scourge of success and a destroyer of personal wealth.

Have you insulated your wealth from these predators?

As a subset of risk management, asset protection planning is what protects your wealth against potential creditors and litigants, children, in-laws, and future ex-spouses. Which strategies work best prove to be very situational.

Asset protection planning is the process of employing risk management products and advanced planning strategies to ensure an individual's or a family's wealth is not unjustly taken.

Moving beyond the astute use of property and casualty and liability insurance, some of the strategies are quite rudimentary and predicated on dissociation (otherwise known as "I don't own it"). That occurs when you transfer your assets to another person or entity while retaining some form of access. Such tactics include moving assets to a spouse and the many versions of offshore trusts and domestic self-settled spendthrift trusts. The law is somewhat developed around the latter as evidenced by the Uniform Fraudulent Transfers Act. As a result, these strategies, if properly executed, will usually oblige a determined opponent to seek a compromise.

More sophisticated approaches to asset protection planning incorporate transformation strategies where your assets are converted into different assets that are much harder, if not impossible, for creditors and litigants to acquire because the assets are protected by state bankruptcy laws. The homestead exemption, interests in limited partnerships or limited liability companies, and the selective use of life insurance and annuities are all examples of transformation tactics. The use of captive insurance companies is also very effective in the right situations.

Research findings. About four out of five business owners are concerned about being involved in unjust lawsuits or being victimized in divorce proceedings (Exhibit 4.9). A lot of this consternation is the result of having been unfairly targeted in lawsuits or knowing people, often other business owners, who have been unfairly targeted in lawsuits. Not only is the potential for loss often exceedingly stressful and problematic, but also there's the commonly intense anxiety over having to go through the experience.

EXHIBIT 4.9:

Concerned About Being Involved in Unjust Lawsuits and/or Divorce Proceedings
% N = 513 BUSINESS OWNERS

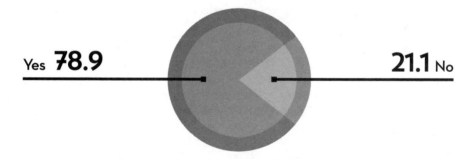

Yes **78.9**   **21.1** No

Of the business owners who are concerned about possible lawsuits and the damage they can inflict, only 15 percent of them have an asset protection plan (Exhibit 4.10). Meanwhile, of the business owners who are concerned and do not have an asset protection plan, three out of five reported that no one explained to them their options in this regard (Exhibit 4.11).

For about a quarter of them, asset protection planning equates with hiding money and other forms of illegality. As we'll discuss in *Chapter 5: Characteristics of Advanced Planning*, every strategy must be well within the boundaries of the law. It's very possible and advisable to protect your wealth by using only those advanced planning strategies that have been carefully vetted and are unquestionably legitimate.

For some business owners, asset protection planning is seen as being either too expensive or too complicated. There's a financial cost to such planning, but it's usually minuscule compared to the cost of not engaging in asset protection planning and being unfairly sued.

EXHIBIT 4.10:
Have an Asset Protection Plan
% N = 405 BUSINESS OWNERS

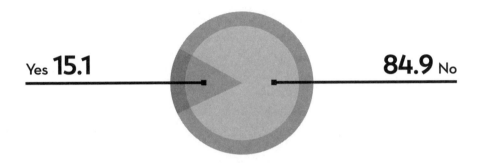

Yes **15.1**   **84.9** No

EXHIBIT 4.11:
Why No Asset Protection Plan
% N = 344 BUSINESS OWNERS

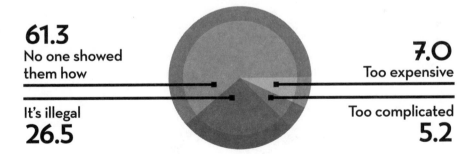

61.3
No one showed
them how

7.0
Too expensive

It's illegal
26.5

Too complicated
5.2

Asset protection planning is certainly a specialty where even many professionals claiming expertise sorely lack real knowledge and skill (see *Chapter 12: Selecting Your High-Caliber Advanced Planner*). Thus, for you to get exceptional insights concerning advanced planning and ensure the strategies are as synergistic as possible, working with a high-caliber advanced planner is essential.

CONCLUSIONS

For business owners, there are tremendous benefits from advanced planning. Because business owners want to protect their wealth, advanced planning strategies are in great demand as they're instrumental in preserving and even, at times, enhancing affluence. They can prove critical to you to extract the greatest benefit from current laws and regulations.

The three types of services—wealth enhancement, estate planning, and asset protection planning—often work in tandem in the hands of a capable advanced planner. Aside from understanding the services, you're better able to make wise decisions by being aware of the criteria for an advanced planning strategy including the role played by the Innovation Process, the topics of the next chapter.

CHAPTER 5

CHARACTERISTICS OF ADVANCED PLANNING

Advanced planning can prove instrumental in enabling you, your family and friends, and your charities to substantially benefit. For an advanced planning strategy to be meaningful and applicable in a particular situation, it needs to meet eight criteria. Furthermore, it's worthwhile that you have a passing understanding of the role creativity plays in the development of new advanced planning strategies.

THE EIGHT CRITERIA OF ADVANCED PLANNING

The preceding chapter discussed the interconnected synergistic services of advanced planning—wealth enhancement, estate planning, and asset protection planning. There are further considerations in advanced planning—each strategy must meet the following eight criteria:

O Flexible

O Discreet

O Transparent

O Coherent

O Risk-sensitive

O Cost-effective

O Complexity-sensitive

O Legitimate

These eight criteria operate best in concert and must be considered in any situation. Let's examine each of them.

FLEXIBLE Advanced planning must be able to change or adapt in order to meet the exigencies of your evolving situation and/or the financial, regulatory, and legal environments. When it comes to these environments, it's inescapable that laws and regulations will be changed, so successful advanced planning has to not only be flexible and informed, but it must also be highly adaptable.

DISCREET A high degree of discretion is a prerequisite between you and any professional with whom you're working. Discretion relates to the nature and details of the interpersonal relationship that is established. Furthermore, though advanced planning strategies are always lawful and morally sound, a low profile can often help avoid unwanted problematic attention.

TRANSPARENT Although there's no interest or benefit for anyone to advertise the intricacies of an advanced planning strategy, the strategy should nonetheless be as transparent as possible. Advanced planning, for instance, is never about hiding or laundering monies; it's about ethically leveraging laws and regulations for your benefit. Any viable advanced planning strategy must be open and available to scrutiny by interested parties such as the government or other professionals.

COHERENT While the three services of advanced planning can be independent of one another—and, indeed, many strategies can work as standalones—a certain degree of integration can and, therefore, should permeate all advanced planning. That is because the strategies carry within them to varying degrees the potential to be used to achieve each of these goals and, as such, they have a bearing on each other and on your planning as a whole.

RISK-SENSITIVE Advanced planning runs along a scale from plain vanilla strategies at one end to the truly esoteric at the other. While every-thing is firmly on the proper side of the legal divide, there's clearly a lot of room to be more or less aggressive. Not surprisingly, many of the most cutting-edge, state-of-the-art strategies are somewhat more aggressive. It's, therefore, crucial that you and your other advisors understand the level of aggressiveness and realize the advantages and disadvantages relative to everyone's risk tolerance (see *Chapter 11: Always Avoid Crossing the Line*).

COST-EFFECTIVE Considering the many state-of-the-art strategies at the disposal of high-caliber advanced planners, there are instances where being on the cutting edge carries too high a price tag. They're just too complicated and expensive, and—bluntly put—unnecessary. Despite the appeal such strategies can have, there are nonetheless times when a more pedestrian yet cost-effective solution is sufficient.

COMPLEXITY-SENSITIVE Many business owners understandably want simple and readily understood solutions to their wealth protection and enhancement issues. Other business owners are willing to consider more intricate and multifaceted strategies. Capable advanced planners are able to provide alternatives geared to the level of complexity you and your other advisors are comfortable with.

LEGITIMATE Needless to say, an advanced plan should never incorporate strategies that are—or that might be perceived as—illegal or even the least bit unethical. Avoiding taxes by skirting the law is out of the question, as is outright tax evasion. Along the same lines, with regard to asset protection, any allegations of fraudulent transfers or any activity that will result in charges of fraud are also out of the question.

Considering how much can be accomplished by staying well within the law, it is only excessive greed, ego, or sheer stupidity that results in otherwise intelligent business owners crossing the line. But with so many shades of gray on the domestic front and even a broader spectrum of gray in the international arena, some very legitimate strategies can seem questionable even though they are not.

What's essential is that every advanced planning strategy you use is a bright-line transaction. That is, there cannot be any question about the legitimacy of the strategy.

As advanced planning is all about having a deep understanding of the laws and regulations along with the ability to actualize solutions, creativity drives the development of new viable and always legitimate strategies. This is known as the Innovation Process.

THE INNOVATION PROCESS

The Innovation Process is the cerebral side of advanced planning. It's where the brainpower of advanced planners and their professional network of specialists (see *Chapter 6: The Virtuous Cycle*) move the industry forward through highly creative thinking. This results in business owners being able to succeed financially in ways that would today seem impossible or improbable.

The Innovation Process starts with evaluating where we are today and concludes with a viable strategy specifically suited to the needs of a select cohort of business owners. The process is in many ways a search for nuance. It's often a matter of identifying a lawful opportunity in the tax code or regulations and knowing under what conditions business owners can use this opportunity to prosper.

The Innovation Process is often about developing methodologies and systems that can turn a breakthrough idea into a viable strategy or even a new financial product. It's predicated on highly specialized expertise, extensive probability testing, meticulous case management, and ethical substantiation. The Innovation Process is comprised of four linked activities ensuring state-of-the-art results (Exhibit 5.1):

o **Environmental scanning** entails evaluating the legal and regulatory landscape and staying abreast of new and emerging industry trends. It also includes analyzing and valuing emerging legal strategies and financial products.

o **Scenario thinking** is envisioning the future based on the data uncovered during environmental scanning. This is also the time when new ideas and concepts are stress-tested.

o **Actualization** is when "maybes" are transformed into workable and usable strategies. This includes validating any financial products that are required for implementation. It also includes developing the back office or technology that's required to realize the strategy.

o **Validation** often takes time. The strategies must be confirmed from a legal and regulatory perspective. Moreover, we strongly believe that all advanced planning strategies must be completely ethically grounded, which is a higher standard than the legal one.

EXHIBIT 5.1:

The Innovation Process

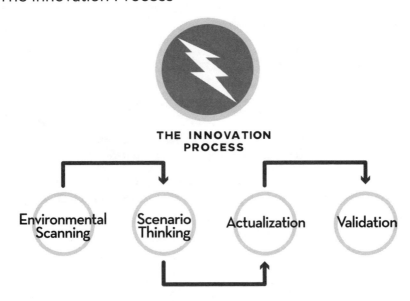

The Innovation Process with solid regularity produces breakthrough ideas and actionable strategies for business owners. Moreover, due to the incredibly dynamic nature of advanced planning, failing to move forward through innovation means moving backwards.

At this moment. What's incredibly important to realize is the value, let alone the viability, of any advanced planning strategy is "time-by-circumstance-sensitive." As advanced planning strategies are predicated on the legal, regulatory, and financial environments that are always in some degree of flux, all the bright-line strategies are practicable and valuable until the lines are drawn differently.

When the tax code is revised, when the regulations are modified, and when the thinking and technology underpinning financial products evolve, then the advanced planning strategies that produce desired results will change. Some may prove more beneficial, others will deliver the same outcomes, and some will become ineffectual.

What's absolutely important to realize is that when it comes to advanced planning, change is inevitable. This means that you need to stay on top of what's happening with the advanced planning strategies you've chosen to implement. You can make certain you're on top of the matter by selecting a high-caliber advanced planner in the first place (see *Chapter 12: Selecting Your High-Caliber Advanced Planner*) and managing the relationship (see *Chapter 13: Working with Your High-Caliber Advanced Planner*).

CONCLUSIONS

Advanced planning is about using fundamental, cutting-edge thinking and strategies to deliver three interrelated synergistic services. Those services are wealth enhancement, estate planning, and asset protection planning. There are eight criteria characterizing advanced planning with a solid and pervasive emphasis on legitimacy. High-caliber advanced planners adhere to ethical standards that are certainly higher than the legal standards.

At the same time, it's important to recognize the critical need for intellectual renewal that translates into new strategies. This is accomplished through the Innovation Process.

The best advanced planners are very systematic and highly process oriented. The Virtuous Cycle, discussed in the next chapter, is ofttimes instrumental to their effectiveness in delivering outstanding results to successful business owners.

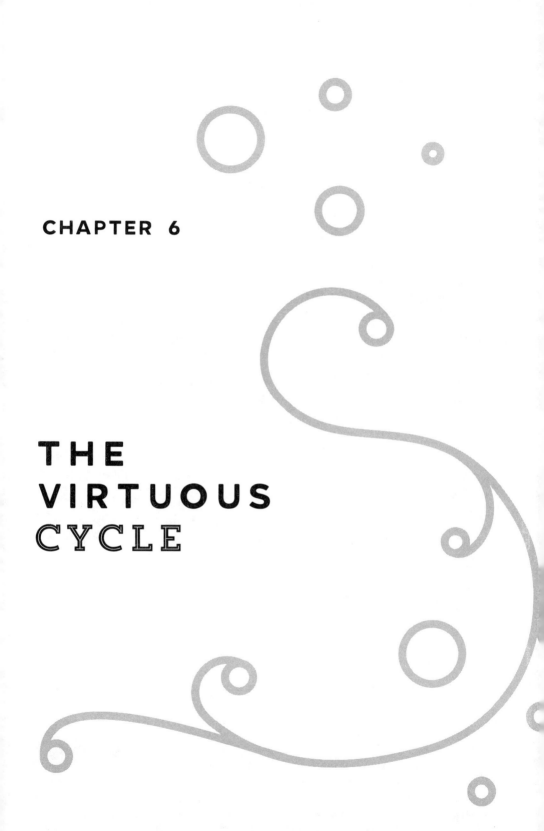

CHAPTER 6

THE
VIRTUOUS
CYCLE

For many leading professionals providing legal and financial expertise, the Virtuous Cycle is a central process of effective advanced planning. It's habitually used by high-caliber advanced planners to enable them to clearly understand their business-owner clients and, consequently, deliver to them the very best thinking and strategies.

The name of this process is based on the fact that it represents the ethical approach and high standards taken by high-caliber advanced planners (i.e., Virtue), and it involves multiple steps (i.e., Cycle). The Virtuous Cycle consists of the steps you and your advanced planner would go through together to identify your concerns, opportunities, and possibilities, and then implement the appropriate strategies.

THE STEPS OF THE VIRTUOUS CYCLE

The Virtuous Cycle is comprised of four distinct steps. Although we present the Virtuous Cycle as sequential, it must be adapted to each business owner's situation often resulting in the need to move back and forth among steps. Continuous feedback from our business-owner clients and their other advisors is a meaningful part of the process in order to make certain we achieve the best results. The phases of the process are (Exhibit 6.1):

○ Profiling

○ **Leveraging the network of specialists**

○ Recommendations and implementation

○ Results and follow-through

EXHIBIT 6.1:

The Virtuous Cycle

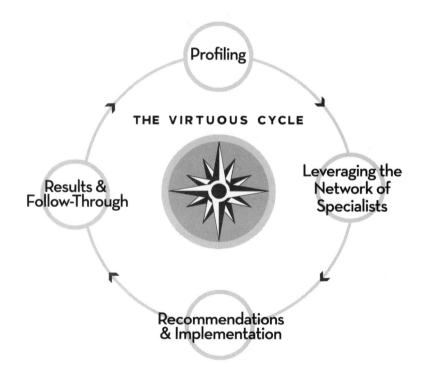

Profiling

Advanced planning requires that your advanced planner have an appropriate understanding of you and your business. While there are literally thousands of profiling tools available to professionals who work with business owners, most of them are severely limited to the considerable detriment of the business owners.

What's regularly required is a more holistic approach when profiling successful business owners in order to be able to deliver superior advanced planning strategies. Probably the most effective and powerful profiling methodology is the *Whole Client Model.*

The Whole Client Model. This profiling methodology has a proven track record and has been adopted by many outstanding professionals and leading financial and legal institutions (Exhibit 6.2). The following seven interdependent sections of the profile are a distillation of the information in an effective structural arrangement:

○ **Client.** Identification of key demographic and psychographic variables.

○ **Goals.** Identification of the business owner's critical issues, concerns, needs, and wants.

○ **Relationships.** Identification of the business owner's personal and professional relationships that matter in conjunction with the extent and the ways they matter.

○ **Financials.** Identification of the business owner's personal and corporate assets and the way his or her personal wealth is presently structured.

○ **Advisors.** Identification of the other professionals who work with the business owners and the expertise and value they each provide.

○ **Process.** Identification of the business owner's preferred method and frequency of interaction and the level of detail required satisfying his or her level of sophistication and curiosity.

○ **Interests.** Identification of those activities and topics that occupy the business owner's time and money, including hobbies, religion, politics, and philanthropy.

EXHIBIT 6.2:

The Whole Client Model

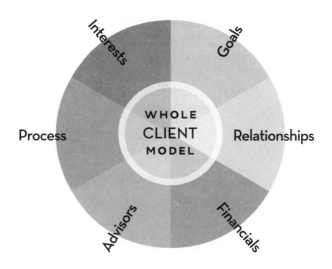

Leveraging the Network of Specialists

Socrates maintained that he was an extremely ignorant man. He held this position despite his great knowledge—or more precisely because of it. He knew how much he did not know.

In order to provide high quality advanced planning strategies, your advanced planner will likely need to leverage a network of niche experts. No one is an advanced planning polymath. There are just too many idiosyncratic, extraordinarily specialized areas of expertise, too much information for any one person—no matter how brilliant—to master. For example, if a successful business owner has both domestic and international business interests, it is probable that the advanced planner will need to network with other professionals who are intimately familiar with the appropriate laws and regulations in some of those jurisdictions. Hence, high-caliber advanced planners turn to niche authorities to supplement their expertise and engage with them in the Innovation Process (see *Chapter 5: Characteristics of Advanced Planning*).

It's not easy to find the right experts. These niche specialists must meet certain criteria including:

○ **They must have the very highest professional standards.**

○ **They must be technical savants and preferably knowledge entrepreneurs.**

○ **They must be able to work well with other exceptionally knowledgeable and thoughtful professionals.**

From the perspective of providing expertise, we've seen a wide variety of talents as part of a professional network. There are nearly always the attorneys and accountants, the life insurance specialists, and the actuaries. Increasingly, management consultants, family business specialists, and psychologists are being included in some of these networks. Still, we find when we look at various networks of specialists there are a fair number of examples of "off the beaten path" participants exemplified by philosophers of various ilk, mystics in a variety of forms, and even one cryptozoologist.

Recommendations & Implementation

This phase of the Virtuous Cycle is where you're presented with possible strategies. This is the culmination of all the work that has gone before. It's these extensively customized strategies that will enable you to achieve your goals and objectives within ethical parameters.

When you decide on an advanced planning strategy, it's time for implementation. This is usually the most straightforward step of the Virtuous Cycle. Compared to the previous steps, it's very mechanical. When it comes to advanced planning, almost always, very mechanical does not equate with easy. Implementation requires an enormous amount of effort and precision.

It's the norm that each advanced planning strategy involves an array of actions usually over time. Obtaining life insurance, for example, can be a complicated and involved endeavor when it comes to meeting the requirements of some business owners. While the decisions concerning the type, amount, and structure of the insurance have been made, the advanced planner must still find the best product at the right price. This often requires the advanced planner to adroitly maneuver through the underwriting process, and, in some circumstances, it might entail creating a fully customized product directly with a re-insurer.

Results & Follow-Through

The advanced planning process is all about results. We don't find business owners really that enraptured by the process, but we do find they're regularly enamored by the results. It's very worthwhile for you and your advanced planner to review the results. This often involves:

○ Reconfirming your profile.

○ Identifying what changes may affect the value of the implemented advanced planning strategies.

○ Setting up the means to monitor and evaluate the results on an ongoing basis.

○ Quantifying the results in monetary terms.

Because of the dynamic and ever evolving nature of advanced planning, it's important to make sure there's follow-through. This means that periodic involvement and continual assessments are critical to ensure you're meeting your goals and objectives. Follow-through usually takes place in three key ways:

○ **Focused applications of the Innovation Process.** As new advanced planning strategies are developed and validated, the advanced planner brings these innovations to your attention.

○ **Self-initiated.** Changes in circumstances will often motivate you or your other advisors to make contact with the advanced planner.

○ **Periodic reviews.** Advanced planning is a subtle discipline in which very small changes can have an enormous effect. This requires that advanced planning strategies be carefully monitored and maintained to continue working effectively.

As the financial and legal world we live in is very dynamic, your use of advanced planning strategies must be so as well. This highlights the importance of advanced planning to be flexible (see *Chapter 5: Characteristics of Advanced Planning*). Consequently, ongoing follow-through is essential.

CONCLUSIONS

The Virtuous Cycle is a highly effective and systematic methodology for delivering optimal advanced planning strategies that are specific to each business owner. In order to get the best results, you must be sufficiently involved in the process to clarify your goals, provide the access and information an advanced planner needs, and take the time to understand the recommended strategies. By employing this approach, high-caliber advanced planners can enable you to get the most effective and productive strategies to meet many of your pressing financial needs and wants.

What we found in our survey of business owners is that few of them are staying current with their planning (see *Chapter 4: Defining Advanced Planning*). This means there are probably numerous opportunities for most business owners to benefit. The real question is: "How can you benefit?"

In the following section, we address various advanced planning strategies. These are just a small sampling of what's available.

PART III

SELECTED
STRATEGIES

DECIDING TO PURSUE AND EXECUTING ADVANCED
PLANNING REQUIRES WORKING WITH TALENTED AND
ETHICAL PROFESSIONALS to determine which strategies are
most appropriate in your unique situation. Consequently, your
advanced planner needs to—individually or in conjunction with
a team of experts—implement the chosen strategies.

The chapters in this section were developed solely to give
you a feel for advanced planning in action. We are not, in any
way, providing a comprehensive review of advanced planning
strategies, nor are we including anything along the lines of
do-it-yourself instructions. Our goal is to help you understand
the possibilities associated with advanced planning and how
they might be helpful to business owners in general and you
and your business in particular. Keep in mind that what works
best for you will depend on your situation, your objectives,
your critical concerns, and your partialities.

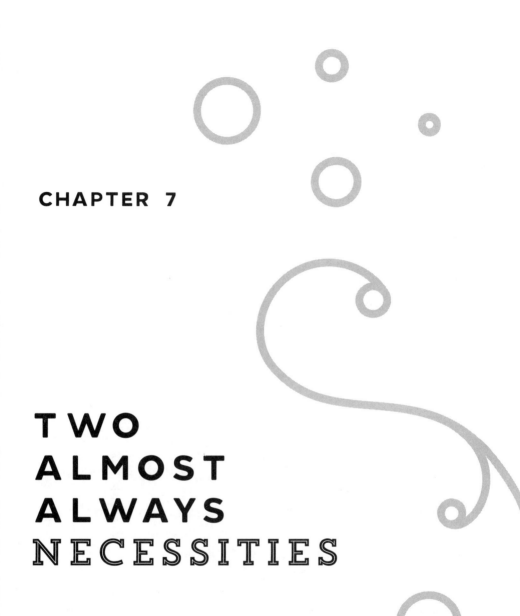

CHAPTER 7

TWO
ALMOST
ALWAYS
NECESSITIES

If something unfortunate happens to you, such as an illness, disability, or even death, there are often many people who want to make sure the business remains viable and that your loved ones benefit from the hard work put into making the business successful. To these ends, there are two strategies you need to put in place:

○ Key person life insurance

○ Buy/sell agreements

These would generally be considered basic strategies. For many business owners, they are fundamental and there's no need to get unnecessarily complex. Still, there are times when sophisticated variations are appropriate as in the case of equity-adjustable hedging strategies and self-financing options using captive insurance companies or premium financing (see *Chapter 8: Solving Problems*).

Keep in mind that straightforward solutions are all that most business owners require. Still, for certain situations, charitable trusts, factoring of accounts receivables, and using private placement life insurance are all more complex ways of addressing key person and partnership concerns. Here, we'll simply discuss the need as opposed to the options.

FOR THAT ESSENTIAL INDIVIDUAL

Key person life insurance is sometimes a necessity. There are a number of times when such insurance is important, such as:

○ **To replace profits or loss of capital due to the death of a critical employee.**

○ **To provide cash to address loan payments.**

○ **To recruit and replace key employees.**

○ **To fund executive benefits.**

The gap. About three out of five of the business owners surveyed have key person life insurance on someone at their company, if not themselves (Exhibit 7.1). In some cases, the life insurance was necessary in order to obtain bank loans. Meanwhile, for those business owners without key person life insurance, almost three-quarters said that if something happened to them or another key employee, the business would fail or be harshly handicapped (Exhibit 7.2).

EXHIBIT 7.1:
Have Key Person Life Insurance
% N = 513 BUSINESS OWNERS

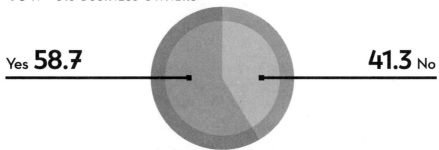

Yes **58.7**   **41.3** No

EXHIBIT 7.2:
The Business Would Suffer
% N = 249 BUSINESS OWNERS

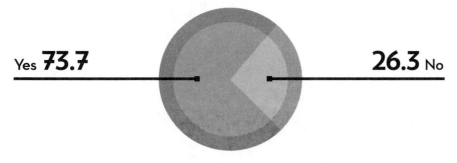

Yes **73.7**   **26.3** No

A further complication is that the key person life insurance was potentially dated and insufficient. In most of these situations, the business owners had not revisited the need for this type of life insurance within the last three years (Exhibit 7.3). Hence, there's a good chance that the key person coverage in place might not be adequate or even properly structured to address the present needs of the company and its owners.

EXHIBIT 7.3:
Reviewed Their Key Person Life Insurance in the Last 3 Years
% N = 249 BUSINESS OWNERS

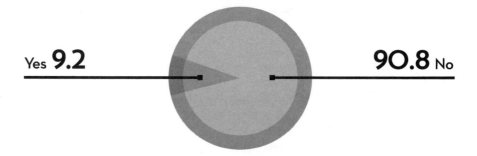

Yes **9.2**　　　　　　　　　　　　　**90.8** No

Aside from key person life insurance, when there are partners in the business, buy/sell agreements are usually very smart to have.

ENSURING A CLEAN SEPARATION

Few business owners want to be in business with the spouses or children of a partner who is no longer able to carry out his or her duties. Severing ties in this type of situation is best accomplished with buy/sell agreements.

When a company has multiple owners and stock that is illiquid because it's privately held, buy/sell agreements are usually an extremely wise planning move. A buy/sell agreement is a legal contract that:

○ **Ensures that when a trigger event occurs, such as the death of an owner, his or her equity in the business will be purchased and the proceeds of the sale will go to his or her heirs.**

○ **Provides a funding source, such as life insurance, to ensure the liquidity needs of the business are met and make sure that the financial demands on the remaining business owners will not be onerous.**

○ **Determines a valuation for a deceased owner's business equity to calculate estate taxes.**

The gap. Having a buy/sell agreement for a privately-held business with multiple owners is very often a sound planning strategy, but not all business owners have them. According to the business owners we surveyed who had partners in their companies (see *Appendix A: Survey of Business Owners*), nearly four out of five had buy/sell agreements (Exhibit 7.4).

EXHIBIT 7.4:

Have a Buy/Sell Agreement
% N = 424 BUSINESS OWNERS

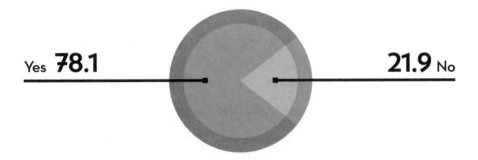

Yes **78.1**   **21.9** No

Death is the most common trigger event written into buy/sell agreements. In fact, few businesses with buy/sell agreements addressed situations other than death. Other possible triggers, such as disability, retirement, divorce, and bankruptcy were largely ignored—an oversight that could later hobble many businesses and partners in those businesses, as the vast majority, if not all, business owners will face one or more of these situations in their lifetimes.

It's problematic that very few business owners have reviewed their buy/sell agreements or their funding mechanisms within the last three years (Exhibit 7.5). Meanwhile, many business owners in the survey reported meaningful changes in the fortunes of their companies making it likely that their buy/sell agreements and funding plans are out of date.

EXHIBIT 7.5:

Reviewed Their Buy/Sell Agreement in the Last 3 Years
% N = 49 BUSINESS OWNERS

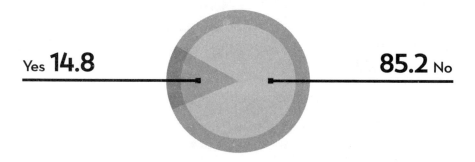

Yes **14.8**   **85.2** No

CONCLUSIONS

What these findings tell us is that many business owners recognize the need for key person life insurance and buy/sell agreements. However, by not monitoring the situation and staying current, there are likely to be complications if something catastrophic were to happen. Mistakenly, for quite a number of business owners, the fact they did something is enough. They have marked them complete on their to-do checklists and forgotten about them.

Some business owners are neglecting or ignoring the adverse scenario that these strategies mitigate. Proper planning, which includes key person life insurance and a funded buy/sell agreement along with keeping the strategies current, will provide timely and cost effective solutions.

There are a plethora of advanced planning strategies that can help successful business owners protect what they've built and pass the maximum value to their loved ones. In the next chapter, we review several important and effective advanced planning strategies.

CHAPTER 8

SOLVING
PROBLEMS

WITH
THOMAS J. RIGGS, MARY PARENTE,
AND CHRISTINE G. PRONEK

There is an arsenal of advanced planning strategies with many of them evolving and improving all the time. More are on the way as a product of the Innovation Process (see *Chapter 5: Characteristics of Advanced Planning*). It's beyond the intent and scope of this primer to address the multitude of strategies. However, we believe it would be beneficial to consider a handful of advanced planning strategies by focusing on their principal benefits—the problems they solve.

Our purpose, moreover, is not to provide a comprehensive review of advanced planning techniques—because, as noted previously, your individual needs, preferences, and situations must be considered in the identification and crafting of the right solutions—rather to offer a "tasting menu" of strategies that represent the type of scenarios and risks that can be addressed with these sophisticated approaches.

OPPORTUNITIES

Advanced planning is effective in addressing a wide array of financial and legal problems. The following are some examples:

- **A real estate developer** is raising money for a venture whereby she will co-invest in commercial properties in the New York metro area with different investors in each property. She wants a liability firewall in place between the properties, and to accomplish that, she was told to place each property in a separate limited liability company. Having numerous limited liability companies, however, generates significant duplicative costs including separate tax return preparation fees, state filing fees, and audit fees. One well-used option is to place all of the properties in a type of special purpose vehicle that allows for unitary financial reporting and tax filing status while maintaining the liability firewall between the properties. This strategy will provide the same liability protection, but will prove less administratively costly.

- **An entrepreneur** has successfully started his business, but now wants to retain and incentivize certain key employees. He feels that awarding equity is the best approach, but he was correctly informed that granting ownership rights directly would constitute current taxable income to the employees. Instead, the entrepreneur can award ownership percentages to the employees utilizing a technique that not only defers taxability to later years, but also results in capital gains treatment.

- **A successful small business owner** has reached the point where she would like to begin the process of passing complete ownership of the business to her children, but she still needs income from the business in order to fund her current living expenses and retirement. She can set up a family business entity that splits the ownership rights into separate components where she retains the income rights while gifting away the control and appreciation/liquidation rights to her heirs. The overall gift and estate tax liability is further reduced through valuation discounting.

- **A business owner** residing in New York City is contemplating the sale of his company. In addition to federal capital gains taxes upon the sale, he is facing state and city income tax liabilities in excess of 10 percent. To help reduce his tax burden, prior to the sale he transfers his closely held shares into a trust in one of several tax-free state jurisdictions. The trust allows for ownership and control to remain with him. The trust then sells the shares incurring no state tax liability.

- **A highly successful business owner** wants to transfer substantially appreciated business assets to his children and grandchildren, but he doesn't want to pay current income taxes or gift taxes on the transfer. He can use installment sales and trusts to transfer assets, allow for a step-up in basis in the hands of his heirs, and defer tax liabilities into the future.

Advanced planning strategies range from basic to increasingly sophisticated. Before going up the scale in complexity, the basics should always be considered. There is a wide variety of advanced planning strategies that can be used by business owners including captive insurance companies, equity stripping, and for the exceptionally wealthy, "floating islands." A few of the more complex strategies that are appropriate for many business owners include:

○ Financed life insurance

○ "Freezing" the value of a business

○ Private placement life insurance

○ Combining private placement life insurance with a charitable trust

FINANCED LIFE INSURANCE

PROBLEM You need to obtain a larger life insurance policy but have limited cash flow.

The essence of premium financing as the term suggests is when the business owner takes out a loan to pay for his or her life insurance policy. There are a number of reasons this can be a wise financial move including:

○ Permanent life insurance policies have a cash surrender value that can provide collateral for a secured loan.

○ There are available life insurance policies offering attractive options for the policy cash value that can diversify the business owner's investment portfolio and outperform the cost of financing premiums.

○ It enables the acquisition of higher face values when there are cash flow concerns.

○ In the U.S., where the annual premium exceeds the annual gift tax exclusion for irrevocable trusts, premium financing outlays can be structured to qualify for the annual gift tax exclusion.

CASE STUDY A 54-year old real estate developer had a need for $25 million of life insurance to fund estate taxes. Most of his cash assets were tied up in his properties. The annual premium to pay the policy outright was a little more than $250,000 per year for his lifetime for a level death benefit policy. In addition, the developer did not have enough annual exclusion beneficiaries, so he would have to pay additional gift taxes on the premiums being paid to the trust that would own the policy.

Since the developer was used to leverage as he had bought many of his properties that way, we looked into a premium finance arrangement. The developer's trust, which would own the policy, was able to borrow the policy premiums from a third party lender. He funded the policy at high levels in order for it to be self-supporting after seven to ten years. Since the policy would be funded at very high levels, the cash value would collateralize most of the loan. The developer would post collateral for any shortfall between the policy cash value and the loan balance. The annual interest charged on the loan could be paid annually or accrued into the loan. This gave him tremendous flexibility for cash flow management.

IMPLICATION. When acquiring life insurance is a wise move, there are times when it makes sound economic sense to finance the premiums. For some business owners, the ability to use leverage to pay the premiums can be financially beneficial.

"FREEZING" THE VALUE OF A BUSINESS

 PROBLEM You want to lower your estate tax bill on the sale of equity in your company.

Locking in the value of your company before a sale or transfer to heirs can be an effective way to minimize taxes. The objective is to "freeze" the value of your business thereby locking in its present value for estate tax calculations. Thus, as the business increases in value, the appreciation is not part of your estate. You're gifting the future appreciation of the business to your heirs.

This advanced planning strategy also proves extremely effective when an older family member wishes to transfer a family business to a younger family member at the lowest possible cost. In fact, sometimes a period of weak performance in the family business provides a terrific opportunity to transfer the business.

If trusts are used to "freeze" the value of the business for estate tax minimization, the strategy can provide the children and even future generations with valuable asset protection. Moreover, it's possible to transfer the wealth to future generations without tax consequences.

There's one advanced planning strategy that is effective in many situations when business owners are looking to sell their companies that locks in the current value of the business thereby eliminating estate taxes on further appreciation. This can be structured to benefit many generations and preserve flexibility. It's a part-sale, part-gift to a trust.

This type of trust puts the assets it holds—all future appreciation of your company—immediately outside your estate. Additionally, you avoid capital gains on the sale to the trust.

CASE STUDY A 60-year old business owner realizes that one of these days he's going to sell the company he founded and built. He has done quite well financially and wants to take care of his children and anticipated grandchildren. Also, he detests taxes. By freezing his business today, he can lower his estate tax bill and move the monies he would otherwise owe the IRS to his family.

The business owner made a gift of $500,000 in stock to a trust and sold another $4.5 million in company stock to the trust. If the value of the company increased by 10 percent per year for nine years and he then sold it, there would be more than $1 million in estate tax savings. Looking ahead, the trust will continue to grow and all the appreciation will pass to the next generation without further taxation.

The business owner could even leverage the tax savings by using a partnership. When using a partnership in conjunction with the trust, he can discount the value of the stock he's transferring to the trust, thereby transferring more monies to his family as opposed to the IRS.

IMPLICATION There are a number of advanced planning strategies that can be employed to "freeze" a business for estate tax purposes. These include various types of trusts as well as partnerships. The best choice is a function of your particular situation. However, for the vast majority of business owners, it makes enormous financial sense to evaluate the benefits and costs of these strategies.

PRIVATE PLACEMENT LIFE INSURANCE

PROBLEM You want to mitigate taxes so you can maximize investment returns.

For more successful and, consequently, wealthier business owners, there are many more advanced planning strategies available. The ability to mitigate taxes when it comes to their personal investments falls into this category.

Investors care more about what they keep, rather than performance numbers. That's why many hedge funds that post big returns can look quite ordinary after taxes are figured. With many hedge funds generating ordinary income and short-term capital gains, federal income tax rates of 39.6 percent will be the norm for most hedge fund investors in 2014. In addition, there's the 3.8

percent net investment income tax. Income taxes in high-tax states such as New York and California could impose at least an additional 12 percent, meaning the combination of state and federal taxes for hedge fund investors could easily exceed 50 percent.

There is, however, at least one way for investors to diminish the tax hit. For over two decades, one of the best-kept secrets in tax planning has been private placement life insurance, which makes it possible for a hedge fund investor to capture returns tax-free. Private placement life insurance is a variable universal life insurance policy that provides cash value appreciation based on a segregated investment account and a life insurance benefit.

Private placement life insurance policies are designed to maximize savings and minimize the death benefit. The investment account can be invested in tax-inefficient hedge fund strategies via an insurance dedicated fund. The death benefit is typically the minimum amount allowed to qualify as insurance under the Internal Revenue Code.

 CASE STUDY A successful businessman with $5 million of investable assets loves his hedge fund investments but realizes more than half of his 2014 profits will go to the federal and state governments.

Comparing the benefits of private placement life insurance to investing in the hedge fund without the life insurance wrapper, there are major differences. Assuming there is a net annual eight percent return, private placement life insurance generates about $5 million more than a taxable hedge fund investment after 10 years. After 20 years, private placement life insurance has outperformed by over $18 million. Held for 40 years, the private placement life insurance policy will produce $120 million more than a taxable account. The superior performance will only increase if the investment returns are higher and/or the tax rates increase.

IMPLICATION Advanced planning can enable business owners to make their money work harder for them by abrogating taxes. By wrapping investments such as hedge funds in life insurance, the money going into the pockets of investors can be dramatically greater.

CHARITABLE TRUSTS AND PRIVATE PLACEMENT LIFE INSURANCE

PROBLEM You want to lessen the income tax impact on an especially large bonus.

Business owners often meet large income tax events with distress, but they're a nice problem to have such as:

○ Large bonuses.

○ Converting a significant IRA to a Roth IRA.

○ Collectors who have sold art or other valuables for a significant profit that will be taxed at the highest federal capital gains rate.

○ Investors who have significant recapture at ordinary income rates upon the sale of an asset.

There are various ways to manage a large income tax liability. Many successful business owners who face this problem have the dual goals of supporting charities they care passionately about and efficiently transferring wealth to their loved ones. For these business owners, the solution is a bright-line transaction incorporating a charitable trust.

A properly structured charitable trust eliminates the federal income tax while transferring significant funds to a charity the business owner has personally selected. If the investments funding the charitable trust perform well, sizable wealth can be transferred to children and other loved ones free of gift and estate taxes.

The type of charitable trust that can be extremely useful in these situations has one significant drawback: The business owner is taxed on all of the income earned in the trust. Without additional planning, all of the charitable trust's income and gains will be taxed. A very effective solution is for the charitable trust to hold a significant portion of its assets in a private placement life insurance policy.

CASE STUDY A business owner is getting a significant bonus: $5 million for facilitating the sale of a part of the company. The business owner would prefer not to pay roughly half of the $5 million to state and federal governments and is passionate about a particular small charity. She also has children she would like to benefit.

She sets up a charitable trust and funds it with the $5 million. Instead of having just $2.5 million remaining after taxes, all $5 million can be used to support her favorite charity. Assuming the charitable trust earns a net return of eight percent annually, the value of the original contribution would more than triple over 20 years. This solution allows the entire bonus to be free of federal income tax, resulting in a much larger charitable gift while also creating a much larger estate for her loved ones that is free of gift and estate taxes. State consequences will vary depending on state tax law limitations on charitable deductions.

IMPLICATION. Combining various advanced planning strategies, such as charitable trusts and private placement life insurance, it's possible to generate enormous benefits for business owners—under the right conditions. As such advanced planning is all about providing solutions.

CONCLUSIONS

We looked at a variety of scenarios where advanced planning strategies can dramatically benefit business owners, and considered a handful of specific strategies.

It's essential to remember that every advanced planning strategy is customized to the particular circumstances of each individual and his or her business. The case studies cited are examples of what can be accomplished with specialized expertise; your situation is likely to be appreciably different. The best strategies for you will be dependent on a variety of unique factors including the structure and value of your assets and your goals. The ideas in this chapter can provide a starting point for exploratory conversations with an advanced planner, an accountant or another advisory professional.

Thomas J. Riggs, JD, CPA, MAS, is a partner of O'Connor Davies and he provides innovative approaches to issues facing family offices, small business owners, hedge fund managers and high net worth individuals. His financial services expertise spans 30 years and includes tax-efficient structuring, business succession and asset protection solutions. He lectures nationally on these and related topics.

Mary Parente, CPA, is a partner of O'Connor Davies and she has over 20 years of specialized experience providing tax compliance and planning services for trusts, estates and high-net-worth individuals. She is experienced in the areas of estate planning and its surrounding disciplines, including advanced fiduciary income tax compliance, trust and estate accountings, and estate administration.

Christine G. Pronek, CPA, MST, is a partner of O'Connor Davies and she specializes in estate planning and estate, trust and gift administration. Ms. Pronek's expertise in this area allows her to advise clients on the preservation and transfer of their wealth in the most efficient manner from the perspectives of both income and estate tax purposes.

CHAPTER 9

RETIREMENT
SOLUTIONS

WITH
TIMOTHY J. DESMOND AND LOUIS F. LIBRANDI

There's a rapidly mounting belief that the goal of attaining financial security in retirement is going to fall squarely on the shoulders of the individual, as certain governmental programs may not be able to deliver as promised. Recent market events have created incredible challenges and unprecedented volatility to businesses and individuals.

Without question, retirement solutions are a wealth enhancement service. They are often a good way to legally shelter assets. There are also times when retirement solutions serve an estate planning function as well.

As we'll see, many business owners are not availing themselves of retirement plans and other ways to maximize their monies down the line. In our experience, we often find there are substantial opportunities for implementing retirement solutions, but many business owners are not yet aware of them.

Before discussing some possible opportunities and retirement solutions, let's consider the findings from our survey of business owners.

RESEARCH FINDINGS

Only about two-fifths of the business owners surveyed have a qualified retirement plan (Exhibit 9.1). These can be either defined contribution or defined benefit plans. Meanwhile, less than one-sixth of them have a non-qualified retirement plan (Exhibit 9.2).

EXHIBIT 9.1:
Have a Qualified Retirement Plan
% N = 513 BUSINESS OWNERS

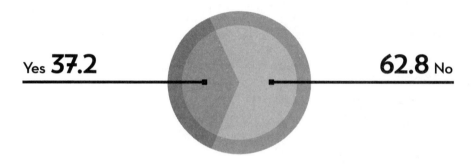

Yes **37.2**   **62.8** No

EXHIBIT 9.2:
Have Non-Qualified Retirement Plan
% N = 513 BUSINESS OWNERS

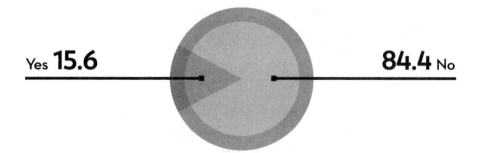

Yes **15.6**   **84.4** No

Among the companies with retirement plans, the monies tend not to be meaningful for the business owners (Exhibit 9.3). Only about 16 percent say these funds are "important." A little more than half report the monies to be "somewhat important." The remaining 28 percent say the monies are "not important." This is

usually a function of the business owners not having significant sums in their qualified retirement plans for any number of reasons such as the plan being "top heavy."

EXHIBIT 9.3:
Importance of Retirement Assets for the Business Owner
% N = 191 BUSINESS OWNERS

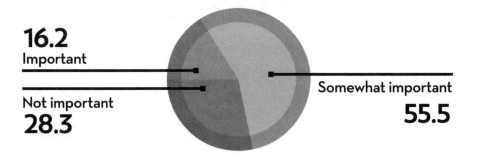

16.2
Important

Not important
28.3

Somewhat important
55.5

At the same time, 322 business owners do not have company retirement plans.
The reason cited by three-fifths of them is cost—such plans are deemed too
expensive (Exhibit 9.4). More than 40 percent of the business owners cite such
plans do not provide them any direct benefits. About 35 percent explain that
difficult business conditions make offering qualified retirement plans unfeasible.
And, almost 30 percent are concerned about liability.

EXHIBIT 9.4:
Reasons for No Qualified Retirement Plan
% N = 322 BUSINESS OWNERS

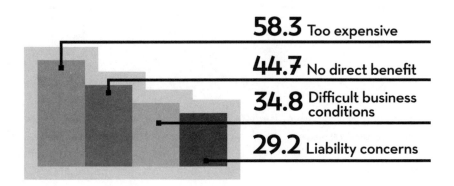

58.3 Too expensive

44.7 No direct benefit

34.8 Difficult business conditions

29.2 Liability concerns

Clearly, many business owners are not availing themselves of qualified retirement plans and as such are missing some very important opportunities.

OPPORTUNITIES

The following is just a small sample of what can be accomplished with respect to retirement planning and qualified retirement plans:

○ **A law firm** pays partners retirement benefits from the general assets of their partnership or a limited liability company. Such firms typically have 401(k) plans that offer minimal benefits. It's possible to provide significant tax deferrals for each partner (from $2 million to $5 million), reduce payroll taxes, provide tax deductible life insurance, and protect capital and retirement benefits in case of bankruptcy.

○ **A start-up private equity firm** tends to use the same structure for management fees and carried interest on investment fund performance. These structures have been in place for 40 years, and Congress is currently focused on increasing taxation on the carried interest. Using different structures today that increase the return on investment for the private equity partner and/or hedge fund manager by 20 percent to 40 percent, assuming the funds have a positive return, are easy to do and make financial sense.

○ **A construction company** has been in business for 50 years and the founder would like to sell the business. However, because the company participated in several multi-employer union defined benefit plans, the business valuation has been significantly reduced because of a $40 million multi-employer repurchase liability. A strategy can be used to mitigate the impact of the repurchase liability along with structures that will offer bankruptcy protection and other benefits.

○ **A small company** has a pension plan that is under funded by $15 million, and it is significantly impacting the business's growth and expansion opportunities. It's possible to enable the business owner to fully fund the pension while fulfilling her business growth and expansion aspirations.

○ **An employee-owned company** has a $23 million repurchase liability with regard to employee retirement obligations. This liability has impacted the growth of the business. It's possible for the company to reduce the impact of the repurchase liability so that the business can continue to grow while meeting the repurchase obligation.

○ **A small business** created an overseas subsidiary a few years ago. As a result, $118 million of profits are trapped in a foreign jurisdiction. If the business repatriates the overseas profits into the U.S., it will pay significant tax in the U.S. on such amount. However, these profits can be brought back into the U.S. without current taxation while allowing for the continued growth of the business on a tax deferred basis.

○ **A small business** has a 401(k) plan that is providing low benefits for the principals, is complex to administer, requires annual reporting and filling requirements, and has fiduciary risk. A strategy can be used that provides the principals better benefits, requires no reporting or filing requirements, and has no fiduciary risk to the principals going forward while offering retirement benefits for workers.

○ **A small business** has a frozen pension plan that is over funded by $17 million because of government funding requirements and market appreciation. The excess assets can be used to improve retirement benefits and be invested in the business going forward on a pre-tax basis.

These examples show just of few of the possibilities that can benefit business owners. Let's now consider a couple of retirement solutions in a little more detail.

DEFINED–BENEFIT QUALIFIED RETIREMENT PLANS

PROBLEM You're looking to get significant retirement benefits from a qualified retirement plan.

We're seeing that many business owners are finding a very strong appeal for certain types of qualified retirement plans. However, the ability of many qualified retirement plans to deliver the value successful business owners are looking for—meaningfully lower taxes coupled with solid benefits for themselves—is sorely lacking. For example, in some situations, as noted above, certain qualified retirement plans, such as 401(k) plans, prove to be top-heavy meaning that the successful business owners are unable to personally receive any real value.

CASE STUDY A 45-year old owner of two successful restaurants with 11 full-time employees and 25 part-time employees is making a lot of money in his businesses and his accountant prompted him to set up a retirement plan. Considering the transient nature of many of his employees, the restaurant owner was looking for a plan where he would be the most significant beneficiary.

He first considered a traditional defined benefit plan. He found he could fund approximately $175,000 a year for himself and the 11 full-time employees. Instead, by choosing a more esoteric defined benefit plan, he is able to contribute and take a tax deduction of about $450,000 for the next ten years with about 90 percent of monies contributed going toward his retirement benefits.

IMPLICATION. Qualified retirement plans are one of the best ways to address the needs of mitigating taxes and creating tax-free growth for business owners. Considering the potential for future increases in taxes, the appeal of qualified plans, especially some of the more sophisticated defined benefit plans, is inclined to rise.

LIFE INSURANCE FOR ESTATE TAXES AND RETIREMENT

PROBLEM You need to pay estate taxes and lack retirement savings or assets.

Business owners often confront a number of financial problems requiring them to make choices about future events. Because of an inability to know the best financial answers decades down the line, advanced planning strategies need to be highly flexible whenever possible (see *Chapter 5: Characteristics of Advanced Planning*).

Many successful business owners are confronting an environment where they'll need to pay estate taxes and need to ensure monies are available in their retirement. While there are various ways to address these potential problems individually, developments in the field of life insurance provide new options including the ability to inexpensively obtain monies to pay estate taxes and/or monies in retirement. The most attractive feature of this strategy is its versatility.

CASE STUDY A 52-year old business owner purchases a life insurance policy with a $10 million face value. He borrows nearly $200,000 per year for 10 years. He pays the interest on the loan averaging out to about $25,000 per year.

The loan is fully paid off in the tenth year. The business owner then receives a tax-free annual income for 20 years—from age 65 to 85—of nearly half a million dollars; combined, this equals nearly $10 million. Meanwhile, the life insurance policy will still provide a death benefit to his heirs of nearly $12 million.

CASE STUDY A 47-year old business owner purchases a life insurance policy providing $48 million of death benefits. She borrows $1.2 million a year for ten years during which the average annual loan interest is about $250,000.

The loan is fully paid off in the tenth year. From the age of 67 to 90, she takes a tax-free annual income of more than $1.5 million. Total tax-free income over the time period will be about $36 million. A death benefit of more than $30 million will still be in place.

IMPLICATION. Advanced planning strategies in the hands of an accomplished professional can be exceedingly powerful. The ability to integrate different approaches results in greater benefits for business owners. In the case study shown here, there are both estate and retirement benefits.

CONCLUSIONS

Retirement solutions tend to address a number of needs and preferences of successful business owners. They are wealth enhancement strategies and can have additional benefits as estate planning and asset protection strategies.

Most business owners are not taking advantage of retirement solutions for a number of reasons including costs, a perceived lack of ability to benefit them directly, an uncertain business environment, and liability concerns. However, a talented advanced planner can probably identify a number of potential retirement solutions that would be highly beneficial to the business owner.

Recognizing that owning a business is usually the best way to create personal wealth and using advanced planning strategies is often a superior way to maximize personal wealth, there's the sometimes complicated matter of finding and working with a high-caliber advanced planner. In *Part IV: Caveat Emptor*, we address this potential sticking point.

Timothy J. Desmond, CPA, is a partner of O'Connor Davies and the Director of the Firm's Employee Benefit Services Group. Mr. Desmond has over 25 years of experience in providing auditing and accounting services to a wide range of industry organizations and employee benefit plans. His main focus is to help employers understand and meet their regulatory compliance requirements and better serve the participants of their respective retirement plans.

Louis F. LiBrandi, EA, ChFC, Fellow CEBSP, TGC, is a principal of the Firm's Employee Benefit Services Group and he has more than 25 years of experience with employee benefit plans. A recognized expert on matters regarding the Form 5500, and on satisfying the many qualification requirements of retirement including 403(b) and 401(k), nonqualified deferred compensation plans, and certain features of welfare/cafeteria arrangements. He frequently represents clients under examination by the IRS and DOL.

PART IV

CAVEAT
EMPTOR

AS A BUSINESS OWNER THERE ARE GOING
TO BE TIMES WHEN ADVANCED PLANNING
STRATEGIES CAN BE VERY USEFUL IN PROTECTING
AND EVEN INCREASING YOUR WEALTH.

In all likelihood, there are strategies you can employ that will
make a significant difference to your net worth. However, your
overall success using advanced planning strategies is not likely
to be determined on the strategies themselves—far from it.

Your ability to benefit by leveraging the legal, regulatory, and
financial expertise to enhance and safeguard your wealth is
almost entirely predicated on your ability to select and work
with a high-caliber advanced planner. The complication is
that a diverse and extensive number of professionals are
extraordinarily interested in doing business with you. Some of
them are liable to be financial predators while other ones are
simply incompetent. Consequently, you must put in the requisite
effort to identify a high-caliber advanced planner and manage
the relationship. This is your most important job in order to
benefit as much as possible from advanced planning.

CHAPTER 10

EVERYONE INTO THE POOL

WITH
MARC L. RINALDI

mong a diverse and extensive number of professionals, the appeal of working with successful business owners is never greater. For a variety of reasons, these professionals recognize the multiple ways they can provide their expertise to business owners and the solid financial returns they'll attain for doing so.

To get a better understanding of why successful business owners are such an appealing prospect, in 2014 we conducted a survey of professionals on the topic.

SURVEY OF PROFESSIONALS

We surveyed six different types of professionals (Exhibit 10.1). More than a quarter of them were investment advisors and a fifth of them were life insurance specialists. Close behind in number were wealth managers and trusts and estates attorneys followed by private bankers and personal accountants.

Exhibit 10.2 summarizes the services provided by each of the types of professionals. The identified services would be considered their core offering. Still, a wealth manager, for instance, can provide financial planning for a fee. What's important to note is that the definition of "primary means of compensation" is that the professional derives 70 percent or more of his or her revenue from the services noted.

EXHIBIT 10.1:

Type of Professional
% N = 807 PROFESSIONALS

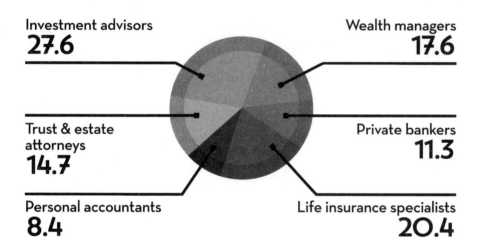

Investment advisors
27.6

Wealth managers
17.6

Trust & estate
attorneys
14.7

Private bankers
11.3

Personal accountants
8.4

Life insurance specialists
20.4

EXHIBIT 10.2:
Service Offerings & Primary Means of Compensation

PROFESSIONAL	SERVICES	PRIMARY MEANS OF COMPENSATION
Trust & estate attorneys	Legal planning	Fees that are either hourly or project based
Investment advisors	Assets under management	Basis point fees
Wealth managers	Multiple financial products	Basis point fees for assets under management and commissions on other products
Private bankers	Assets under management and credit	Basis point fee for assets being managed and interest for credit services
Life insurance specialists	Sale of life insurance and annuities	Fees and commissions
Personal accountants	Tax planning, bill paying, and bookkeeping	Fees that are either hourly, retainer, or project based

To be included in the survey, the professional had to meet the following two criteria:

1. **A personal average annual income over the previous three years of $300,000 or more. This is a proxy representing a minimum level of capability and accomplishment.**

2. **A focus on the affluent with a strong desire to build a more substantial practice.**

One of the most pronounced findings from this study is that professionals are operating in an exceptionally competitive environment.

INTENSE COMPETITION

One of the more important themes that emerged from this study is that more than seven out of ten of the professionals—across the board—would define their business environment as very or extremely competitive (Exhibit 10.3). The rest report the business environment to be competitive. No professional said his or her business environment wasn't competitive.

EXHIBIT 10.3:
Level of Competition
% N = 807 PROFESSIONALS

● VERY OR EXTREMELY COMPETITIVE

● COMPETITIVE

Very or Extremely Competitive	Competitive	
79.0	21.0	Trust & estate attorneys
73.5	26.5	Investment advisors
64.8	35.2	Wealth managers
81.3	18.7	Private bankers
68.9	31.1	Life insurance specialists
67.6	32.4	Personal accountants
72.2	27.8	Weighted Average

There are a number of interconnected reasons for the perceptions of intense competition including:

○ **The commoditization of professional services.** There's nothing unique that a professional can provide and a similarly talented and knowledgeable professional cannot. Professional services have become commodities. This doesn't mean that certain professionals aren't more adept at delivering their expertise and working with business owners, for this is in fact the case. It's just that, in the final analysis, they're fungible.

○ **The unrelenting boom in the number of professionals entering their respective fields.** The incredible growth in the number of practitioners in various fields is unabating. While relatively few of these professionals are going to excel, they tend to create "noise" resulting in more competitive pressure.

○ **The progressively limited financial returns possible with less successful clients.** While it's possible to make a living working with less successful clients, there are serious limitations to a professional's practice doing well. As such, the focus of the preponderance of professionals is to concentrate on more successful clients such as business owners.

○ **The snowballing effect of technology resulting in the greater marginalization of many professionals.** Technology is doing a great job of streamlining the work of professionals and sometimes replacing them. Consequently, professionals gravitate to clients where technology is relatively less intrusive in their practices such as business owners.

○ **The expansion of services provided by many professionals encroaches on the offerings of previously strategic partners.** For a number of reasons, by design, many professionals are choosing to offer a broader array of services. The result is that they're expanding into more practice areas which can alienate strategic partners and increases the level of competition all around.

All this competitive pressure results in:

○ Professionals making a greater push to find and work with successful business owners.

○ A tendency among some professionals to adopt looser moral standards (see *Chapter 11: Always Avoid Crossing the Line*).

As a result, many professionals have given significant thought to what it will take to build a successful practice.

ACHIEVING SUCCESS

Considering the big picture, for professionals to be more successful they need to control their costs while generating greater revenues. No surprise here. While costs tend to often be controllable, the real and more demanding issue is how to generate more revenues. The unquestionable answer for most professionals is in sourcing and doing more with high-quality clients.

More high-quality clients. More than nine out of ten of the professionals surveyed report that finding more high-quality clients for their offerings is instrumental and essential to their success (Exhibit 10.4). This sentiment is consistent with decades of similar research we've conducted with a broad cross-section of financial and legal professionals regarding their future plans and impediments to success: *accessing new high-quality clients is their number one issue.*

EXHIBIT 10.4:

More High-Quality Clients are Critical to Future Success
% N = 807 PROFESSIONALS

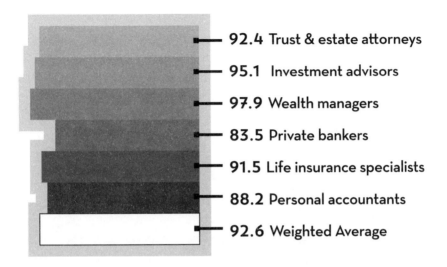

92.4 Trust & estate attorneys

95.1 Investment advisors

97.9 Wealth managers

83.5 Private bankers

91.5 Life insurance specialists

88.2 Personal accountants

92.6 Weighted Average

Additional business per high-quality client. About a third of these professionals identify the importance of repeat business or expanded business to building a very successful and profitable practice (Exhibit 10.5). By repeat business, we're referring to the client coming back to address other concerns and issues. Expanded business entails more of the same services with the same clients.

What is not included here is a continuation of the services being provided to a high-quality client. For example, if an investment manager is managing $2 million for a business owner and that client doesn't add more monies to the account, then this is not considered repeat or expanded business (even if the account appreciates).

Many of the trust and estate attorneys and life insurance specialists, for example, are transaction oriented. Therefore, they don't see many, if any, opportunities with existing clients. It's not uncommon for some professionals—investment advisors, private bankers, and personal accountants—to believe they have all the business (e.g., investable assets or tax work) from high-quality clients. While this might be the case, it's not always so.

EXHIBIT 10.5:
More Business with Current Affluent Clients is Critical to Success
% N = 807 PROFESSIONALS

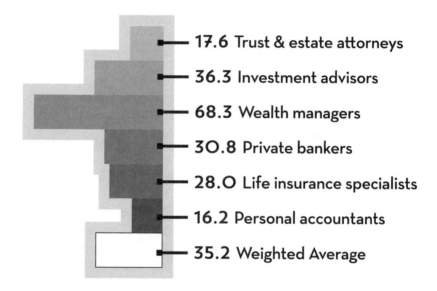

17.6 Trust & estate attorneys

36.3 Investment advisors

68.3 Wealth managers

30.8 Private bankers

28.0 Life insurance specialists

16.2 Personal accountants

35.2 Weighted Average

In sum, across the board, new high-quality clients are considered essential for a highly successful practice. For slightly more than a third of the professionals surveyed, another critical factor to their success is their ability to provide additional and sometimes different expertise to their high-quality clients.

SUCCESSFUL BUSINESS OWNERS TO THE RESCUE

When it comes to defining who is a high-quality client, about three-quarters of the professionals surveyed report that successful business owners perfectly fit the bill (Exhibit 10.6). This sentiment is most pronounced among life insurance specialists and trust and estate attorneys. It's least prominent among investment advisors, as many business owners have limited discretionary assets. However, there are regularly substantial assets in their companies' retirement plans that can benefit from talented investment professionals.

EXHIBIT 10.6:

Successful Business Owners are High-Quality Clients
% N = 807 PROFESSIONALS

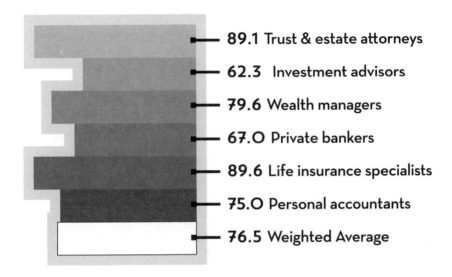

- **89.1** Trust & estate attorneys
- **62.3** Investment advisors
- **79.6** Wealth managers
- **67.0** Private bankers
- **89.6** Life insurance specialists
- **75.0** Personal accountants
- **76.5** Weighted Average

What this means is that, overall, various types of professionals are looking at business owners and often their businesses as the type of client they very much want to work with. They're the high-quality clients that can result in the success of a professional's practice. Unfortunately, the fact that business owners are high-quality clients for a broad array of professionals brings out the financial predators coupled with a legion of incompetents with less skills and knowledge.

CONCLUSIONS

Professionals face a decidedly competitive environment that is generally seen as only likely to get worse. This is potentially driving down incomes forcing them to scramble more than before and concentrate their efforts where there are the greatest possible returns. In many respects, business owners have the needs, wants, and preferences as well as the financial resources that work so well for various professionals. Evidently, this is the reason *everyone is jumping into the pool.*

When it comes to advanced planning, the competition for successful business owners can, unfortunately, result in business owners being unduly pressured, exploited, and cheated. Furthermore, there's the very strong possibility of less than capable professionals seizing any opportunity and, consequently, destroying wealth with unsound strategies, poor execution, and impractical experience.

We've repeatedly emphasized the need to maintain the highest ethical standards. So, before addressing how to find and work with high-caliber advanced planners, in the next chapter we look for the proverbial line in the sand with the intent to never cross it.

Marc L. Rinaldi, CPA, is the Partner-in-Charge of Financial Services for O'Connor Davies. He is a leader in the field of investment, portfolio and investment partnership accounting. His alternative investment experience includes valuation, due diligence, performance reporting and risk management for family offices, private equity, private foundations and endowments.

CHAPTER 11

ALWAYS
AVOID
CROSSING
THE LINE

hat would some people do to save $10 million or more in taxes? What would a person do to keep her wealth out of the hands of a lunatic soon-to-be ex-spouse? As it turns out, many business owners and the professionals they employ will sometimes take substantial risks to maintain or enhance their affluence, even when those risks and actions are legally questionable and ethically indefensible.

There's a great demand for services that enable taxes to be evaded, just as there's a great demand for services to protect and even hide assets. At the same time, regrettably, there are many unscrupulous professionals who are more than willing to assist on these fronts with the expectation of being well compensated for their efforts.

Because advanced planning can involve sophisticated strategies and necessitate highly specialized expertise, it's fairly easy for successful business owners to find themselves moving quickly beyond the legal limits especially when paired with bad guidance. Just consider the example of abusive trusts.

ABUSIVE TRUSTS

Abusive trust schemes are built on the creation of a number of trusts that hold selected assets and/or income streams. By vertically layering these trusts, fraudulent expenses can be charged to subsequent trusts resulting in a decrease in taxable income. Another use is to create the illusion of separation of control in order to protect the assets in the trusts. There are many ways to structure abusive trusts. The following are some rudimentary examples:

- **The abusive asset management company.** An asset management company formed as a trust is created with the individual appointed as the director, although an advisor is designated the trustee and is responsible for running the asset management company. This often is the start of the layering process.

- **The abusive business trust.** The individual transfers a business to a trust and in return receives certificates or units of beneficial interest. The business trust makes payments to the unit holders so that the business trust does not have to pay any taxes. The business trust can also be set up so that future estate taxes are avoided.

- **The abusive private annuity trust.** The individual sells appreciated property to a trust in exchange for an annuity, which, in turn, sells the assets and reinvests the money. The individual claims recognition of the built-in gain over his or her life, and the trust is not included in the estate.

- **The abusive family residence trust.** The individual transfers his or her family residence to a trust and receives units that are claimed to be part of a taxable exchange resulting in a stepped-up basis for the property. The trust is thus in the rental business and claims to rent the residence back to the owner who does not pay rent as they are identified as caretakers of the property.

- **The abusive final trust.** When a number of abusive trusts are being employed, some individuals create a final trust that holds the trust units of other abusive trusts and is the distributor of their income.

Abusive trusts come in a wide variety of forms with all of them interconnected and clearly being used for illegal purposes. It's a form of the matryoshka principle where one doll is hidden within a similar doll. By analogy, unless all the dolls are opened, you cannot find the only one that isn't hollow.

Meanwhile, there are a multitude of scenarios where it's quite easy to be misinformed and go over the line, let alone intentionally move outside the law. This is sometimes the case with offshore trusts.

OFFSHORE TRUSTS

In spite of what many promoters of offshore trusts and accounts profess, there are few legitimate uses of offshore trusts if you seek to lower your income taxes. This is certainly the case when offshore trusts are established solely to hide earnings. Too often, however, offshore trusts are over-promoted as financial panaceas by shady advisors.

To enhance their attractiveness, certain offshore jurisdictions have mutated the trust and corporation concept with both positive and negative results. Unfortunately, there are more than a few professionals who fail to recognize the issues and potential complications of using offshore trusts.

While offshore trusts do indeed serve a purpose and can prove beneficial, they're far from the magical cure-alls many promoters make them out to be. They can serve valid purposes for business owners. However, it's all too common for many who use them to do so inappropriately with potentially disastrous results.

BEING OVERLY AGGRESSIVE CAN LEAD TO DISASTER

Moving away from the black zone of clearly illegal acts, many business owners enter the far more complicated gray zone where the legality of a given strategy is open to interpretation. This is the dominion where a professional's integrity or lack thereof becomes readily apparent.

Simply because a "friendly" attorney is willing to give the "right" answer as evidenced by a favorable private letter ruling, it doesn't mean that such an opinion abrogates the relevant legal considerations and the pertinent moral issues involved in the strategy. In effect, because some professionals are morally malleable doesn't rescind the business owner's responsibility in the eyes of the law.

Given the many shades of gray, how do you know when an advanced planning strategy, especially a complex one, crosses the line of legality? How aggressive is too aggressive?

A clear indicator for when a strategy is too aggressive is if its sole economic benefit that's not explicitly governmentally sanctioned is to enable a successful business owner to pay fewer taxes and serve no other economic function, or is used to blatantly dodge legitimate creditors. In the former case, the business owner is likely engaging in tax laundering; in the latter, the business owner is probably illegally hiding money. For the advanced planning strategy to be a bright-line transaction, in every case, there has to be a socially sanctioned business reason to implement the strategy.

A PERSONAL NOTE

We know the limits—the legal and ethical limits—with the latter being a higher standard. Most importantly, we're not at all interested in moving beyond the ethical limits. We believe there is an absolute need to view all potential advanced planning strategies through a "righteous lens."

We sometimes find successful business owners coming to us to implement strategies they've heard about. When we carefully evaluate these strategies, we find, with great regularity, they go too far—they cross the line. Many we deem to be illegitimate. Some are possibly legitimate but turn on obscure phrasing in the tax law, for instance, where the intent of the law is clearly being sidestepped.

With advanced planning, there are many ways for business owners to enhance and protect their wealth. Hence, we never act foolishly and instead show these business owners legally and ethically acceptable ways to best accomplish their goals. If they insist on pursuing inappropriate strategies, we part company immediately.

CONCLUSIONS

Saving money, particularly on taxes, is a rational and legitimate priority for many business owners—and for the professionals who want to work with them. Given the amount of money involved for successful business owners, and the amount of money and business at stake for these professionals, new strategies are constantly being devised (see *Chapter 5: Characteristics of Advanced Planning*).

While some of these strategies are legal and morally sound, others are either illegal, unethical, or so clearly conceived to circumvent established laws that they will soon be adjudged illegal. It's the advanced planner's responsibility to draw the line at the edge of ethically validated innovation rather than take a risk however measured that could jeopardize a business owner's wealth, livelihood, and even freedom. It's the business owner's responsibility to select a high-caliber advanced planner and manage the relationship, which are the focus of the next two chapters.

CHAPTER 12

SELECTING YOUR HIGH-CALIBER ADVANCED PLANNER

Advanced planning is not as we practice it very common among financial and legal professionals. In many, many ways, it proves to be more the exception than the norm. This is a function of our intense focus on being state-of-the-art and having a strong client-centered orientation coupled with unquestionably high ethical standards.

Finding and working with a high-caliber advanced planner can be arduous, so it pays to be skeptical. Without a doubt, for you to attain the myriad and significant advantages of advanced planning, you must carefully choose the advanced planners with whom to work.

> **When it comes to benefiting from advanced planning, selecting a high-caliber advanced planner is many times the most important decision you're going to make.**

But, choosing an exceptional advanced planner isn't enough. It's also extremely important to know how to work effectively with an advanced planner thereby enabling you to garner the greatest benefits from the relationship (see *Chapter 13: Working with Your High-Caliber Advanced Planner*).

MISTAKES WERE MADE

Business owners like everyone else want to work with the "best" legal and financial professionals—people at the top of their respective fields. From their own experiences and those of other business owners they know, it is clear that ofttimes the "best" were not hired. In fact, this is a pervasive situation proving to be highly detrimental to business owners. Nearly three-quarters of the business owners surveyed reported they themselves or business owners they know have hired less than capable professionals (Exhibit 12.1). And, almost one-quarter of business owners they know have been taken advantage of by advisors they employed (Exhibit 12.2).

EXHIBIT 12.1:
Have Hired Less than Capable Professionals
% N = 513 BUSINESS OWNERS

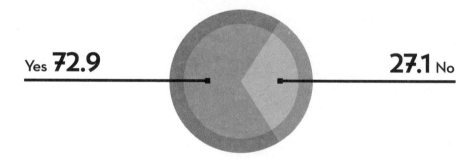

Yes **72.9**   **27.1** No

EXHIBIT 12.2:
Taken Advantage of by Professionals
% N = 513 BUSINESS OWNERS

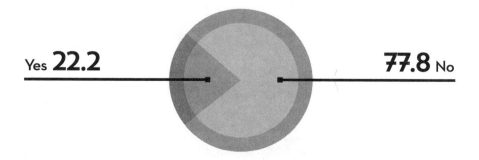

Yes **22.2**   **77.8** No

While these findings pertain to a broad cross-section of advisory professionals and are not limited to advanced planners, the implication for selecting an advanced planner is clear. Essential to getting the best advice is the ability to wisely identify expert, morally sound professionals with whom to work. This makes the astute selection of these authorities critical to your ability to preserve or enhance your wealth.

Some business owners are quite adept at sourcing and managing talented professionals. At the same time, we've consistently found that when business owners are educated on the processes that enable them to make better decisions in these contexts, their effectiveness at sourcing, selecting, and benefitting from professionals can increase exponentially. As noted, your ability to work productively with these professionals is also a critical function and discussed in the next chapter.

FIVE CRITERIA FOR SELECTING A HIGH-CALIBER ADVANCED PLANNER

It's very difficult to evaluate the professional competencies of legal or financial authorities. Your asset protection plan, for instance, can be determined to work only if you're in the unfortunate position of being taken to court. And if it doesn't work, then it's too late. Consequently, there are five critical criteria you should be attentive to when selecting an advanced planner. They are:

CRITERION #1 Proven integrity

CRITERION #2 Operational transparency

CRITERION #3 Extensive technical expertise

CRITERION #4 Access to niche experts

CRITERION #5 Sensitivity to and experience with business owners

By carefully using these criteria to screen prospective advanced planners, you'll be more effective and better able to avoid the legion of financial and legal advisors who are looking to exploit you or are simply not up to the job.

CRITERION #1 PROVEN INTEGRITY

Integrity is at the very top of the list. To protect or enhance the wealth created by successful business owners, the advanced planner must be scrupulously honest.

For business owners, the very nature of dealing with preserving wealth results in becoming a target for a plethora of morally bankrupt advisors—financial predators. There often seem to be more financial predators targeting successful business owners than there are honest, attentive, capable professionals. With the complexity of many advanced planning strategies, coupled with the strong appeal of paying less taxes or keeping money out of the hands of fraudulent creditors, it's often fairly easy for a financial predator to swoop in and decimate the hard-earned wealth of a successful business owner.

You must, consequently, take considerable care when evaluating an advanced planner. The following two questions can prove instrumental in helping you evaluate the integrity of any financial or legal professional, and they've proven especially important in evaluating an advanced planner.

QUESTION #1 "Under what conditions would you fire a client?" **When business owners insist on taking actions that are beyond the limits, the advanced planner should fire them.**

Possible follow-up questions include:

○ Have you ever fired a client?

○ Can you give me an example of a situation where you fired a client?

○ How did you handle it?

QUESTION #2 "What will you NOT do?" The objective of this question is for you to determine where the advanced planner sets his or her limits.

Possible follow-up questions include:

○ Have you ever been asked to do something you considered inappropriate?

○ Can you give me an example of a situation where someone came to you with an inappropriate request?

○ How did you handle it?

As noted, with both these questions, it's very useful to have the advanced planner provide examples, as it's highly likely they've had the unfortunate experiences of having to fire a client and being approached with illegal or unethical requests. You want to get as good a feel as possible about the veracity and genuineness of the advanced planner. This is why so many business owners turn to the professionals they have a good and trusting relationship with to find a high-caliber advanced planner (see below).

It's so very important that every advanced planning strategy you use is a bright-line strategy being executed by a knowledgeable, talented, and exceedingly ethical advanced planner. Just bear in mind that as tax laws change, for example, the viability and even the legitimacy of various strategies can change, which is why advanced planning needs to be highly adaptable (see *Chapter 5: Characteristics of Advanced Planning*).

CRITERION #2
OPERATIONAL TRANSPARENCY

As noted in *Chapter 5: Characteristics of Advanced Planning*, transparency is a defining quality of advanced planning. While it's advisable to be discreet concerning the use of some strategies, this doesn't mean advanced planners—including the brilliant and talented ones—are involved in some sort of conspiracy. Far from it. It's really just a matter of avoiding undue attention.

What's essential when selecting an advanced planner is that he or she is completely open and forthright with you. What you should always require is operational transparency. This takes a number of forms including being very clear about the compensation arrangements and the right to obtain second opinions, third opinions—whatever you want—in addition to verifying the advanced planner and the viability of the strategies proposed. For example, the following are usually glaring red flags:

○ **Requesting you sign a hold harmless agreement.** This would abrogate the professionals of any liability you incur due to the strategy they executed on your behalf. So, if you're penalized for using a strategy, the professionals who recommended and implemented it are legally off the hook for any of your problems that occur because you followed their advice.

○ **Requesting you sign a nondisclosure agreement.** After signing such an agreement, you're unable to share the strategy with other professionals. This makes it impossible for you to get outside confirmation on the legitimacy and efficacy of the strategy. Very often, this type of agreement is both a way to make it impossible to discover you're about to be cheated while simultaneously being effective as part of a cunning way to push a questionable sale.

There are no good reasons for you to have to sign either a hold harmless agreement or a nondisclosure agreement. If you do sign such agreements, you're likely putting yourself at a potentially serious disadvantage. What these agreements do is protect unscrupulous professionals while they may very well place you at serious risk.

Another aspect of operational transparency is fee clarity. More specifically, how does the advanced planner you're evaluating get remunerated. There are only a few possibilities, and you need to be aware and comfortable with them. They include:

○ Hourly, retainer, or project fees

○ Fees based on assets or net worth or a portion thereof

○ Contingent fees

○ Statutory as well as negotiable commissions on financial products

○ Some combination of the above

There is no "best" compensation arrangement. Some of this is a function of the type of professional hired, others are based on the client's comfort level. What is very important is being cognizant of the compensation arrangements, understanding the logic of the arrangements, and being very comfortable with the arrangements.

Being aware of how you and the advanced planner are going to work together along with your other advisors is often a necessary component of a meaningful relationship. Some of the issues to consider include:

○ Who is your primary or lead professional, and why?

○ How is information going to be shared among your various professionals, and how is this process going to be monitored and controlled?

○ What are the preferred approaches to addressing technical disagreements, discrepancies, and intellectual differences?

○ When your other advisors require education with respect to advanced planning strategies, how does this impact overall costs?

Clearly, your understanding of how an advanced planner will work with you and your current team of professionals before committing to an engagement will likely make the relationship that much more productive.

CRITERION #3
EXTENSIVE TECHNICAL EXPERTISE

Everyone wants to work with a top-notch professional. Discounting the fact that there are a slew of financial and legal predators looking to economically ravage successful business owners, another problem is finding a talented and knowledgeable advanced planner.

There are many professionals who are just not up to the job of delivering viable advanced planning strategies. In a survey of 227 self-identified asset protection attorneys, we found that few of them were indeed knowledgeable about many asset protection strategies (Exhibit 12.3). Only about a sixth said they were leading authorities on the subject. Furthermore, about three-quarters admitted they need to become more knowledgeable with respect to asset protection strategies.

EXHIBIT 12.3:

Delivering Asset Protection Expertise
% N = 227 SELF-IDENTIFIED ASSET PROTECTION LAWYERS

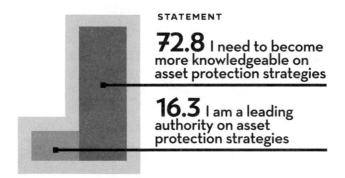

STATEMENT

72.8 I need to become more knowledgeable on asset protection strategies

16.3 I am a leading authority on asset protection strategies

We also found that many of these self-identified asset protection attorneys were not abreast of some of the more common strategies in the field (Exhibit 12.4). They were knowledgeable concerning the more basic asset protection strategies but not some of the more esoteric ones.

EXHIBIT 12.4:

Familiar with Specific Asset Protection Strategies

% N = 227 SELF-IDENTIFIED ASSET PROTECTION LAWYERS

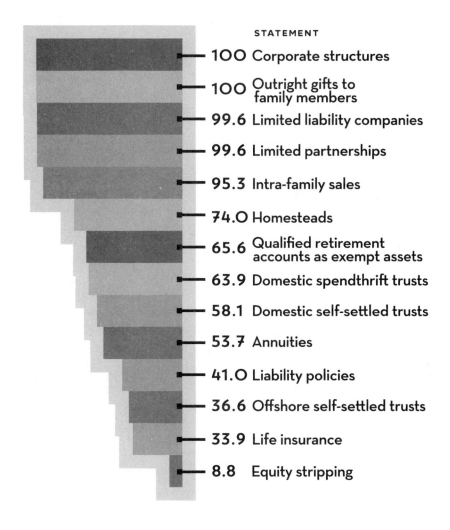

STATEMENT

100 Corporate structures

100 Outright gifts to family members

99.6 Limited liability companies

99.6 Limited partnerships

95.3 Intra-family sales

74.0 Homesteads

65.6 Qualified retirement accounts as exempt assets

63.9 Domestic spendthrift trusts

58.1 Domestic self-settled trusts

53.7 Annuities

41.0 Liability policies

36.6 Offshore self-settled trusts

33.9 Life insurance

8.8 Equity stripping

Just because a professional proclaims expertise in advanced planning, this might not be the case. You need to consider numerous factors in order to effectively evaluate the technical competence of an advanced planner, including:

○ Educational background

○ Professional experience

○ Professional licenses and designations

○ Association with industry organizations

○ Publications and speaking engagements

○ Recognition from peers in the financial and legal communities

From a technical perspective, many of the very best advanced planners are knowledge entrepreneurs. They're at the cutting-edge of their field contributing to its advancement. These advanced planners are immersed in the Innovation Process (see *Chapter 5: Characteristics of Advanced Planning*). Moreover, they're very willing to share their expertise and insights with their peers.

CRITERION #4
ACCESS TO NICHE EXPERTS

As we noted in *Chapter 6: The Virtuous Cycle*, there are no advanced planning polymaths even when they're knowledge entrepreneurs. While some situations will not call for expertise beyond what your advanced planner is able to do, there are times when highly specialized expertise is required.

At these times, what's needed is a team of niche specialists to help develop and implement customized advanced planning strategies for businesses and their owners. It's generally useful for you to be aware of the network of niche experts available to your advanced planner. Some of the questions you should consider are:

○ Who are the niche specialists?

○ Why did your advanced planner choose them?

○ What are their areas of expertise?

○ What are their credentials and backgrounds?

○ How does everyone work together?

○ How is everyone compensated?

By having even a rudimentary understanding of the depth and breath of your advanced planner's network of niche specialists, you'll be better able to gauge his or her capabilities. Also, if you need to interact with the niche experts, it's important you understand their roles and what they bring to the table.

CRITERION #5
SENSITIVITY TO AND EXPERIENCE WITH BUSINESS OWNERS

For advanced planners to be effective, they must understand the goals, objectives, financials, and so forth of their business-owner clients. When appropriate, the advanced planner will have to be willing to expend the time and effort to learn what is required to deliver state-of-the-art customized strategies. Consequently, the Virtuous Cycle is central and it's why the Whole Client Model plays a critical role in the process (see *Chapter 6: The Virtuous Cycle*).

In choosing an advanced planner, you want to look for one who is indeed attentive to the needs and preferences of business owners. Moreover, as you work with your advanced planner, it's essential that he or she is appropriately focused and responsive (see *Chapter 13: Working with Your High-Caliber Advanced Planner*).

Business owners are a distinct type of client. Their working environments and financial affairs are entirely different than other accomplished clients such as celebrities or corporate executives. Clearly, advanced planning is applicable to all manner of successful and wealthy individuals and families. However, the particularities, the idiosyncrasies, the characteristics of the business owner's world make it essential that they work with advanced planners who are attuned to their issues and concerns, their problems and opportunities.

An advanced planner's experience in the field is essential. Understanding the professional's background and the background of the other professionals supporting him or her is very, very important. In effect, a track record of achievements and proven technical proficiencies are something you must determine and absolutely insist upon.

Your goal is to find a high-caliber advanced planner, not a financial predator or an incompetent. Hence, it's important to understand how successful business owners effectively source talented, knowledgeable, and morally sound professionals.

HOW BUSINESS OWNERS FIND QUALITY FINANCIAL AND LEGAL PROFESSIONALS

There are a number of ways business owners identify advanced planners with whom to work. Some of these ways are synergistic providing reinforcement and confirmation as to whom to select. The way business owners source high-caliber advanced planners is in line with how they source most high-end professionals. Thus, these findings can prove useful in your efforts to find a high-caliber advanced planner.

When it comes to sourcing top quality professionals—and high-caliber advanced planners would fit in here—the principal way is by referral from another capable and trusted professional (Exhibit 12.6). In fact, more than four out of five business owners report turning to professionals they're currently engaging—whom they consider capable and ethical—when it comes to finding another professional for their business or help them address personal matters. This makes sense on a lot of levels.

EXHIBIT 12.6:
Likely Ways to Find a New Professional to Work With
% N = 513 BUSINESS OWNERS

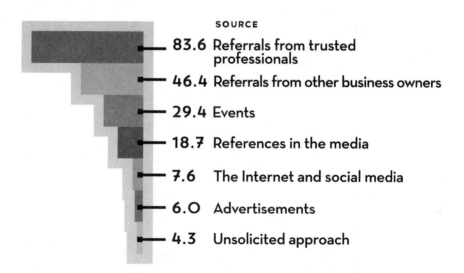

SOURCE

83.6 Referrals from trusted professionals

46.4 Referrals from other business owners

29.4 Events

18.7 References in the media

7.6 The Internet and social media

6.0 Advertisements

4.3 Unsolicited approach

Top-flight professionals are aware of other adept, responsible, and ethical experts and are able to critically evaluate their proficiencies and likelihood of fitting well with their business-owner clients. Relying on trusted and proven experts to source new professionals is an excellent risk reduction strategy for business owners as the introducer's credibility and professional relationship with the business owner is on the line.

This finding is exceedingly consistent whenever it comes to how people access high-end professionals. It doesn't matter the nature of the situation. Whether it's finding the best physician or the best management consultant or the best advanced planner, when it becomes too difficult to evaluate services and expertise, turning to professionals for referrals in whom you have confidence is usually the best solution.

About half the business owners reported referrals from their peers is the way they sometimes source new professionals. This is very often a function of the perceived similarity of business issues and the degree of respect a business owner has for another business owner's assessment and judgment.

Almost 30 percent of the business owners reported that they found some of the professionals they ended up hiring at events. These are most often educational breakfast or lunch meetings, workshops, and conferences. Two critical factors play into the viability of these types of events:

○ **The stature and credibility of the people putting on the event.**
The reputation and standing of those producing the event are at risk if the professionals they're inviting you to hear are less than exceptional.

○ **The stature and credibility of the professionals speaking at the event.**
The more the presenters are knowledge entrepreneurs, for instance, the more likely you'll find value in the event.

Almost a fifth of the business owners said that those professionals repeatedly cited in the media—newspapers, magazines, and other people's blogs—are ones they consider when selecting a professional. The recognition these professionals receive is seen as validating them. However, there are two caveats:

○ **The quoted comments of the professionals have to be meaningful.**
It's not enough that a professional is quoted. He or she has to say something that resonates.

○ **The professional has to be quoted with some degree of regularity.**
When reporters and bloggers are motivated to return consistently to a professional source, it validates their expertise, creativity, and reliability.

All the other ways a business owner can source a professional are not very well used. However, it's very likely that these other methods interact and support one another or help validate selection decisions. While many business owners are probably going to follow referrals they get from the professionals with whom they're presently working and already respect, other positive feedback and high-visibility can all contribute to the selection decision.

CONCLUSIONS

Whether it's because of financial predators or incompetents, business owners can lose a great deal in their effort to protect or enhance their wealth. Moreover, successful business owners are habitually targeted by the immoral and incapable.

When you're seeking the expertise of an advanced planner, you'll probably be inclined—like many business owners—to rely principally on referrals from the professionals you're currently using and feel good about. This is a smart way of taking a lot of the risk out of the selection decision. Even so, it's imperative that you take an active approach to choosing an advanced planner, and we advocate you use the five criteria discussed.

After choosing an advanced planner, you still have to make sure that the relationship works well and meets your needs. The only way to ensure that the relationship operates smoothly is to maintain control—it's your money; it's your responsibility.

CHAPTER 13

WORKING WITH YOUR HIGH-CALIBER ADVANCED PLANNER

While sourcing a high-caliber advanced planner is critical, it's also likely to be insufficient. You must also constructively manage your relationship with your advanced planner to get optimal results.

Simply, you must know what you're paying for and what results you're going to get. The complication is that effectively working with an advanced planner takes effort on both your parts. Moreover, you must be 100 percent confident as to the moral exactitude of your advanced planner at all times.

It's far too common for these relationships to be less than satisfying for the business owner. This need not be the case.

GETTING WHAT YOU WANT ISN'T ALWAYS EASY

In looking at the quality of the relationships many business owners have with the financial and legal professionals they've employed, there tend to be problems. We found that nearly four out of five of the business owners surveyed reported being uncomfortable and unhappy working with some of the financial and legal professionals they've engaged (Exhibit 13.1).

EXHIBIT 13.1:

Uncomfortable and Unhappy With Some Professional Working Relationships

% N = 513 BUSINESS OWNERS

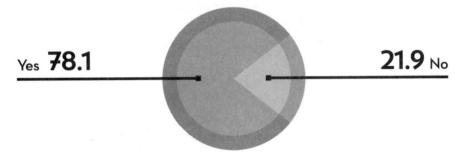

Yes **78.1**   **21.9** No

The consequences of a poor working relationship is that somewhere along the way you're going to be shortchanged. Not necessarily in the sense of being outright cheated, but your frustration and the accompanying stress and tension is going to translate into wasted time and effort, squandered monies, recriminations, and very importantly, missed opportunities.

There are a number of reasons for this disconnect. Using a statistical technique called factor analysis, we were able to discern the major and multiple problems with the professional relationships that proved unfruitful (Exhibit 13.2). Many of these reasons feed and reinforce each other. For example, a professional who provides esoteric, mystifying explanations and is unresponsive is more inclined to be perceived as arrogant.

EXHIBIT 13.2:

Reasons for the Discontent
% N = 404 BUSINESS OWNERS

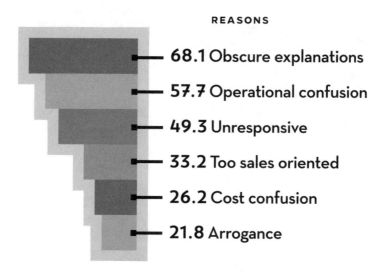

REASONS

68.1 Obscure explanations

57.7 Operational confusion

49.3 Unresponsive

33.2 Too sales oriented

26.2 Cost confusion

21.8 Arrogance

Let's consider each of these reasons in greater detail in addition to some possible ways to correct the problems.

OBSCURE EXPLANATIONS

The number one factor producing consternation among business owners is the inability of professionals to communicate effectively. For all the education and knowledge these experts possess, they often do an amazing job of making everything excessively complicated and befuddling. It's probably because of their extensive training and laser-like focus on technical details that they forget to tailor their remarks for their audience.

By analogy, most business owners are not interested in how a watch works, but rather its ability to accurately tell time. For example, almost 65 percent of business owners want to only know the results of a tax strategy (Exhibit 13.3). Another 30 percent are interested in the fundamentals of tax strategies they're considering. Less than one in ten are concerned with the details of the tax strategy. Nevertheless, it's not uncommon for attorneys, accountants, and other tax specialists to go into mind-numbing and abstruse details on the mechanics of a tax strategy causing rifts with their clients and other advisors.

EXHIBIT 13.3:
Level of Detail of a Tax Strategy
% N = 513 BUSINESS OWNERS

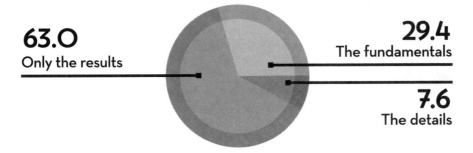

63.0
Only the results

29.4
The fundamentals

7.6
The details

Whether they need to make themselves feel or look smart, or addressing the technical minutia is a crutch, or they're just incapable of taking sophisticated strategies and communicating their essence, a goodly number of professionals are pretty inept at explaining the value and rudimentary processes of various advanced planning strategies. So many of them disregard their audience—the business owner and his or her other advisors—derailing the opportunity for all involved.

Solutions include:

○ Make sure the advantages and disadvantages of any advanced planning strategy you're considering are clearly spelled out in ways you understand.

○ Keep asking questions and continue to request further clarification until you're truly comfortable.

○ Be clear about the timing and steps involved in implementing any selected advanced planning strategy.

It's essential that you have a basic understanding of the results of an advanced planning strategy together with any potential complications that might arise with their antidotes. Moreover, your other advisors must have an even greater level of understanding. To make sure this happens, you must own and oversee the process.

OPERATIONAL CONFUSION

It's all too characteristic of professionals to fail to communicate the way they're able to deliver their expertise. Their clients often don't understand what is expected of them or the way the professional needs to function or what the deliverables are going to be. All this operational confusion results in some very unhappy clients.

While you aim to get insights into how an advanced planner works and will work with you before you engage (see *Chapter 12: Selecting Your High-Caliber Advanced Planner*), very often it's not until you're actually working with the expert that you will encounter complications. Unfortunately, this is more the norm than the exception. The issue is not that there are going to be some glitches in the working arrangement, but that you manage the relationship to your satisfaction.

Because of the nature and aims of advanced planning (see *Chapter 4: Defining Advanced Planning; Chapter 5: Characteristics of Advanced Planning*), the potential for misperceptions and mix-ups is considerable. For example, it's often necessary for an advanced planner to bring in niche specialists (see *Chapter 6: The Virtuous Cycle; Chapter 12: Selecting Your High-Caliber Advanced Planner*), which tends to add to the operational confusion. Who these experts are and how they work with the advanced planner and you can be a source of consternation.

Along the same lines, advanced planning is a process of incremental steps (see *Chapter 6: The Virtuous Cycle*). Without being aware of these steps in conjunction with the need for refinement in determining and implementing an advanced planning strategy, business owners can be easily put off.

Solutions include:

○ **Making certain you understand the rationale for the information you're asked to provide including how that information will be used.**

○ **Understanding how the relationship and planning process should work such as the logic and steps involved in the Virtuous Cycle.**

○ **Knowing the deliverables you should expect and how you can judge their effectiveness.**

Advanced planning strategies can be used to solve some very thorny matters. In delivering such expertise, there's a great deal of potential for operational confusion and their accompanying adverse consequences. To mitigate such potential problems requires you bear down and be very clear and comfortable with how the ongoing relationship between you and the advanced planner will work.

UNRESPONSIVE

For about half of the unhappy business owners, a major driver of their discontent is when professionals are not being appropriately responsive. Examples of this include:

○ **They miss deadlines that were set by you, them, or a third-party like the tax authorities or other governmental agencies.**

○ **You're not responded to in a timely manner even as the professional professes to be very attentive and client-centered.**

○ **They're not addressing the issues that are most pressing and important to you and are, instead, talking about themselves and their services.**

A large part of the issue is the perception that the professionals are not really listening. The impression is that they're too busy and wrapped up in other matters to pay attention as they should.

Solutions include:

○ **Clearly setting the parameters—the limits and bounds—of your professional relationship.**

○ **Determining and communicating the nature and level of contact and under what conditions changes will need to be made.**

○ **Specifying the response times you expect when making inquiries and holding the professional to these deadlines.**

Almost by definition, a hallmark of professionalism is responsiveness. When the professionals you engage fail to be appropriately reactive, it's likely an indicator of a poor relationship and muddled priorities. When it comes to delivering advanced planning strategies, such behavior is unacceptable.

TOO SALES ORIENTED AND COST CONFUSION

About a third of the business owners surveyed felt that professionals they engaged were much too intent on closing business and making sure they're being paid instead of dealing with their concerns. In effect, these business owners saw some professionals as being overly pushy and focused on their own compensation as opposed to helping solve financial and legal problems.

At the same time, about a quarter of the business owners are confused about the costs of the legal and financial services. The problem can become ever more convoluted when costs are a function of time as in the case of those billing hourly. You need to believe that the advanced planner with whom you're working is not just trying to sell to you and that he or she is willing and able to make the costs transparent.

Solutions include:

○ **Know how the professionals you've engaged are being compensated.**

○ **Know the industry-based ranges of compensation professionals receive for similar expertise.**

○ **Negotiate the compensation arrangement whenever possible.**

When it comes to advanced planning, it's all about getting meaningful ethically-sound results. If someone is pushing an advanced planning strategy on you, it's a pretty fair bet that you're being oversold. The situation is further complicated when you're unsure how much it's all going to cost. Again, in these situations it's time to find a new professional.

ARROGANCE

About a fifth of the business owners surveyed reported having worked with professionals that exuded arrogance. In effect, some of the business owners felt they were looked down upon by some of the professionals they hired. This perception is highly correlated with the other reasons business owners are unhappy and uncomfortable with professionals they've engaged.

The solution here is simple and straightforward: if taking charge of the relationship with the recommended solutions noted above does not improve the advanced planner's attitude and behavior toward you, then you should fire that individual and find a caring professional with whom to work.

CONCLUSIONS

Advanced planning can produce seriously great results for many business owners. This means you have to first find a very capable and ethical advanced planner. However, even sourcing such a capable and worldly professional isn't enough. You must also be able to work cooperatively and productively with him or her.

It's fairly common for business owners to have less than good experiences with some of the professionals they employ. What's essential is that you maintain control and provide direction in the relationship. This way, you'll get the outcomes you're looking for and have a positive experience. The solutions provided above are a solid step in the right direction.

PART V

BEING
WEALTHY

RUNNING AND POSSIBLY SELLING A SUCCESSFUL
BUSINESS CAN POTENTIALLY MAKE YOU QUITE WEALTHY.
Considerable monies very often open up new doors and create
new issues. Maintaining and possibly growing your fortune will
likely be a consideration. With the boom in private wealth,
there's been a parallel boom in family offices. While a single-
family office or a multi-family office might not make sense
for you, it's probably worthwhile to understand what they
are and what they do.

Along the same lines, many of the wealthy are philanthropically
motivated. With significant wealth you have more options when
it comes to the people and causes to support and the way
you go about distributing funds. For many of the very wealthy,
private foundations—principally because of the control
they provide, though there are many other benefits—
are a serious consideration.

With family offices, you're focused primarily on your
immediate world. With private foundations, you're focused
on some segment of the broader world.

CHAPTER 14

THE
FAMILY OFFICE
OPTION

BY
RUSS ALAN PRINCE, HANNAH SHAW GROVE,
AND GEMMA LEDDY

A pronounced trend among the wealthiest people in the world is creating a family office to have the expert, dedicated resources to optimally manage their wealth, finances, and family matters. If you do manage to join the ranks of the financial elite, then you'll have the opportunity to consider your own family office or using the services of a multi-family office. Let's begin by considering these two types of family offices.

TYPES OF FAMILY OFFICES

While there are many variations, basically, there are two types of family offices—single-family and multi-family offices. In general, a single-family office is an organizational structure that manages the financial and personal affairs of ONE wealthy family. Because a single-family office is driven purely by the needs and preferences of the underlying family, there is no standard for how it should be structured.

Some single-family offices are lean enterprises focusing exclusively on investing with a skeleton crew while others are much more robust organizations with in-house staff, numerous vendor relationships, and a broad platform of services. This disparity means it's difficult to establish hard-and-fast criteria for how a single-family office should be defined other than its dedication to a sole family. Though it remains unclear, estimates of the number of single-family offices range from a few thousand to more than ten thousand.

In contrast, a multi-family office structure is a business that aims to build deep and long lasting relationships with affluent clients. The multi-family office seeks to provide highly customized solutions, specialized expertise, and responsive service.

Many kinds of entities identify themselves as multi-family offices creating an expansive field of disparate contenders. Though today's multi-family offices often come from dissimilar backgrounds—some were single-family offices looking to share infrastructure costs, others were small groups of like-minded families who saw an opportunity to expand, and still others were commercial entities that chose to focus narrowly on the needs of the ultra-wealthy—now they are organizations with common attributes and are run, more often than not, with an eye toward profit and growth.

New organizational structures for family offices are emerging that are geared specifically around the needs of a wealthy sub-segment. Just consider the following examples:

- **The hub-and-spoke single-family office.** When offspring or different branches of the family want to invest independently, but want the multitude of other benefits that the original family office can provide, a single-family office can adopt a hub-and-spoke-model. This model can be adapted to address several different scenarios; one example: the "spoke" is the new entity operated by the child who is running or overseeing his or her portfolio and the "hub" is the parent's family office providing all the other deliverables (see below).

- **The celebrity multi-family office.** Entertainers and athletes have very specific financial needs due to limited career longevity and the monetization potential of their brand capital. Some multi-family offices have incorporated expertise to address the unique requirements and preferences of celebrities in addition to providing them with creative ways to enhance their wealth.

○ **The virtual single-family office.** This model draws on technology-based solutions and the connectivity of the Internet to allow a handful of employees to manage a cadre of outsourced experts on behalf of a family. As technology and user-interfaces become more advanced, and more specialists and experts become available on a freelance basis, it is likely that more families, especially young wealth and digital natives, will choose the virtual single-family office due to its cost efficiency and operational appeal.

While there will remain two basic types of family offices, it's clear that a good number of variations are on the horizon, and new iterations will continue to emerge as needs and perspectives evolve.

DELIVERABLES

Family offices, writ large, tend to provide two principal categories of services: those that relate to managing wealth and those that relate to family support (Exhibit 14.1). Under the umbrella of wealth management, we often find investment management, advanced planning, and private investment banking. Simultaneously, we often see administrative and lifestyle services under support services. Let's consider these various services.

EXHIBIT 14.1:
Family Office Deliverables

WEALTH MANAGEMENT			SUPPORT SERVICES	
Investing	Advanced Planning	Private Investment Banking	Administrative	Lifestyle
Traditional asset management • Asset allocation • Manager selection • In-house investments Alternative investments • Hedge funds • Private equity	Wealth enhancement Estate planning Asset protection planning	Buying and selling interests in businesses and other assets Capital raising • Sourcing bank loans • Sourcing investors	Data aggregation Bill paying Tax preparation or coordination Acting as the day-to-day CFO Reporting and recordkeeping	Family security Concierge services Medical concierge Philanthropic advisory Formal family education Managing fine art/collectibles Property management

○ **Investment management.** Whether selecting specific investments or choosing money managers, a critical role of most family offices is addressing the wealthy family's investable assets. Included here are "traditional investments" coupled with alternatives such as hedge funds and private equity. A strong suit of many family offices is that they take a comprehensive approach to investment management, which includes addressing tax considerations. Some family offices handle all the portfolio construction and management themselves, while others establish the investment policy and use a committee to select outside managers and monitor their performance against objectives. Either way, most family offices are organized around this function to some degree.

○ **Advanced planning.** Larger and more established family offices are highly attuned to state-of-the-art advanced planning strategies (see *Part II: Advanced Planning; Part III: Selected Strategies*) to help them ensure that their assets are ideally structured and protected and will pass in the most tax efficient way to the beneficiaries and causes of their choice. Significant wealth is more complex and allows for a greater variety of strategies and structures to be deployed, which is frequently a critical advantage for specialists working in or for family offices. Due to the extraordinarily wide range of objectives that can be addressed through advanced planning strategies, most family offices accomplish their goals using a combination of in-house and outsourced expertise.

○ **Private investment banking.** More than ever, the very wealthy are interested in buying and selling major assets such as operating companies, real estate, or intellectual property. Family offices are, therefore, often integrated into the acquisition and divestment processes in order to ensure that appropriate levels of attention have been given to any transaction and that the families' wealth is always being maximized (see *Appendix B: Maximizing Personal Wealth When Selling Your Business*). Investment banking capabilities are typically sourced on an as-needed basis and can also be used to raise capital and find investors.

○ **Administrative services.** Helping a family and its family office run smoothly calls for a range of administrative functions and services. These can include everything from organizing files and documents to paying bills, preparing and coordinating taxes, recordkeeping and reporting, managing employees and the associated human resources activities, and monitoring and evaluating investment performance. In essence, administrative services provide the backbone of a family office's operations and can have far reaching implications about the entity's transparency, agility, and effectiveness.

○ **Lifestyle services.** This is a catch-all category that includes the activities not directly related to finances and wealth management; frequently, they are activities that have more to do with lifestyle support and ensuring the safety and enjoyment of individual family members. They can include services and support requiring ongoing involvement and coordination, such as private security detail, a medical concierge where the providers are integrated in the day-to-day routines of clients, or special projects of varying durations such as overseeing a custom design and construction project or researching and engaging college admissions specialists.

There are no right or wrong answers for the range of services a family chooses to include in its family office. Which specific services a particular family office will provide are determined by the needs, wants, and preferences of the wealthy families involved. This, in turn, leads to a vast number of variations in the offerings. More important than the array of deliverables is the nature of the experience a family office provides the very wealthy.

THE FAMILY OFFICE EXPERIENCE

A major advantage of the family office model is its holistic approach to meeting the demands and desires of wealthy families. By taking a holistic approach, family offices are able to connect the dots between services and initiatives more effectively for their charges than most independent professionals could if they were engaged directly. By having a more comprehensive understanding, the family office is able to deliver superior solutions to wealthy families.

Another characteristic of the family office model is the degree of attention it pays to family members. With a quality family office, the level of responsiveness cannot be surpassed. Furthermore, by being both holistic and having the finest service model, family offices are often able to anticipate the family's needs and wants thereby providing a yet higher level of attention.

The ideal experience is a topic around which family office employees and family members can find common ground. In a recent survey of ultra-affluent individuals, we asked about the enduring and increasing appeal of multi-family offices. They told us that they closely link the following qualities—high responsiveness, customized solutions, extensive financial expertise, holistic approach, and product neutrality—with the multi-family office structure and mission and, importantly, find them lacking in relationships with most large-scale banks and brokerage firms.

All told, for the wealthy family, the family office experience is usually astoundingly positive—the epitome of caring, capable, and comprehensive service dedicated to the family and customized around their needs.

KEY CONSIDERATIONS

The benefits of having a family office can be exceptional, and the degree of control and privacy achieved through a single-family office can rarely be duplicated with another type of structure or relationship. But there is a trade-off required to successfully establish and operate such an entity. Single-family offices are discrete organizations and not regulated by the Securities and Exchange Commission or any other government or civil agency, which means that they (and the families who establish and own them) are entirely responsible for their own procedures, controls, and staff. This, in turn, can mean you have a large, complex business on your hands that is expensive to run and maintain.

Some of the things you should consider before committing to this course of action include:

○ **Involvement and oversight.** How much day-to-day involvement do you and the other principal family members want? Do you want to be consulted on every decision or would you prefer being part of a governing board or a committee that meets periodically to set strategy and assess progress?

○ **Infrastructure requirements.** What functions are necessary for your office and how will they need to be staffed? Do they require any special equipment, licenses, or materials?

○ **Compliance and risk management.** Will you have the internal controls in place to ensure compliance with federal and state laws and regulations surrounding securities and investments, employment, banking and lending, trust, taxes, and other relevant areas?

○ **Business continuity and insurance.** What are your plans to ensure that the office's critical functions will continue if there is a personnel issue or damage to the property or systems? How will you ensure that all human and capital resources are protected?

○ **Staff members.** How many full-time and part-time staff do you anticipate needing? Will they be employees of the family office or an operating company? Are you prepared to offer benefits and a safe work environment to them? Will you cover the expenses associated with continuing education for their professional designations?

○ **Outsourcing and partnerships.** How will you source and vet potential providers? Who will manage the relationships?

○ **Cost analysis.** Do you have a clear sense of the cost to build and maintain such an organization? Is the annual cost of running a structure that entails all the necessary functions acceptable? Is it worth spending to achieve your goals?

Creating the legal structures to house a family office and its assorted functions is a relatively simple process, but having the entity operate smoothly and efficiently on a daily basis requires significant oversight and involvement. We have frequently seen families let things inadvertently slip through the cracks as their financial and personal affairs become more extensive, more disparate, and more complex. It's not uncommon, for instance, to find:

O **Families with multiple homes in different countries and tax jurisdictions can easily fall behind in tax payments and appropriate insurance coverage.**

O **Mail can end up in two or three places simultaneously meaning correspondence and tax documentation may never get to the addressee.**

O **Inventories of assets can be outdated making it difficult to report accurately on holdings, file taxes, update insurance policies or file claims, or conduct accurate valuations.**

O **Estate planning and succession documents are drafted but not implemented or remain unfunded essentially leaving the family, its assets, and its intentions exposed.**

In addition to unexpected and unintended lapses like the ones described family offices must evolve in lockstep with the family members they support. Collectively, this means that family offices must easily adapt to changing demands and new opportunities. Fortunately, many family office providers are structured in ways that enable them to work in concert with (rather than replacing) an existing effort.

Depending on your unique circumstances and preferences, you can upgrade your service providers to bring in higher levels of niche expertise, add new outsourcing partners with specific discipline experience, or create an alliance with a multi-family office that will backfill your operations with their resources. All of these scenarios will help increase your family's bandwidth and expertise while allowing you to maintain a desirable degree of control and confidentiality.

THREE TRENDS IN THE FAMILY OFFICE UNIVERSE

The world of family offices continues to progress. The following three related trends are making family offices ever more appealing to the wealthy.

O **The number of family offices and the amounts of money they oversee will multiply.** There appears to be a direct relationship between the cumulative amount of private wealth and the number of both single-family and multi-family offices. With the boom in private wealth creation, we're finding a corresponding boom in family offices. This is because the advantages of family offices are so persuasive.

○ **The bar for deliverables will continue to rise.** While the numbers of family offices continue to increase, the quality of their offerings will also increase. This is very similar to the Innovation Process in advanced planning (see *Chapter 5: Characteristics of Advanced Planning*). The wealthy rightfully demand the latest thinking and optimal opportunities, and family offices must rise to the occasion.

○ **The pace of new innovations in family office structures will intensify.** The shifting environment for personal wealth creation will result in more structural variations in family offices. They will become more and more customized to the unique situations of the wealthy families they serve. This is both a function of demand as well as technological advancements.

These and other emerging trends will continue to reshape the universe of family offices and the opportunities available to the financial elite. Family offices must constantly adapt and find ways to innovate and trail blaze in order to stay relevant and valuable to their clientele, the most prized and powerful cohort in the world.

CONCLUSIONS

As we've stated numerous times already, owning a business or something of value is the most common and reliable way to create private wealth. When your equity stake is monetized, there's a good chance that you'll want to understand the options available to help you manage and sustain your newfound fortune. The family office option—whether it's establishing your own single-family office or becoming one of a select clientele of a multi-family office—and the model of comprehensive, customized, and dedicated service is proving to be the preferred option for the exceptionally affluent.

In the meantime, there are a number of actions you can take now that will help structure and position your assets for the highest possible valuation, sales price, and retained amount, all with an eye toward maintaining and growing your personal wealth.

Gemma Leddy, CPA, is a partner of O'Connor Davies and the Director of its Family Office Practice. She has over 25 years of experience in public accounting and the private sector. Ms. Leddy and the Firm's Family Office Group provide comprehensive financial management, advanced planning and CFO services to high-net-worth individuals, family offices, executives, entrepreneurs and their businesses.

CHAPTER 15

CONSIDERING A PRIVATE FOUNDATION

BY
WITH THOMAS F. BLANEY AND
CHRISTOPHER D. PETERMANN

Successful business owners are often quite philanthropic. As noted in *Chapter 1: The Roads to Riches*, almost 70 percent of those surveyed expressed a desire to be more charitable. The monies they amass from their business achievements are a great way to fund worthwhile not-for-profit institutions and causes.

There are many ways to give to charity. The most common is referred to as "checkbook philanthropy." This is where you write checks (cash also works very well) to the not-for-profits you care about. The use of charitable trusts can also be highly effective (see *Chapter 8: Solving Problems*). However, when you become seriously wealthy, you'll very likely consider establishing and running your own private foundation.

WHAT IS A PRIVATE FOUNDATION?

A private foundation is a not-for-profit organization (i.e., charity) that's primarily funded by a person, or family, or a corporation. The largest assets in a private foundation are usually investments that produce income. The income is used to support the operation of the private foundation and, most importantly, make grants to other organizations.

SETTING UP AND RUNNING YOUR FOUNDATION

There are a number of steps you must take when establishing a private foundation. You'll need to make numerous decisions along the way. For some of these decisions, you're well served by working with a quality professional. Let's look at the steps:

○ **Decide on the structure of your private foundation.** The two basic choices are a charitable trust or a not-for profit corporation. There are advantages and disadvantages to each.

○ **Determine purpose and grant-making guidelines.** These decisions provide a guide to how your private foundation will operate. They're also instrumental in getting tax-exempt status.

○ **Obtain an employer identification number.** This number will be used to identify your private foundation for tax purposes. It's similar to a social security number for individuals.

○ **File organizing documents.** All the appropriate forms have to be filed with the Internal Revenue Service. Once the Internal Revenue Service approves your private foundation, you may need to file with your home state to adhere to regulatory guidelines.

Setting up a private foundation can be an intricate and involved process as can the ongoing management of your private foundation. In this regard, running a private foundation is very much like running a business. Detailed accounting and the filing of tax returns are required. A variety of experts are usually needed such as legal and accounting professionals to handle regulatory and compliance matters. If you're overseeing the assets of the private foundation, investment professionals will regularly be engaged.

WHY CREATE A PRIVATE FOUNDATION

While there are certainly costs associated with creating and managing a private foundation, there are distinct benefits for doing so. There are many reasons people create private foundations. Three of the most pronounced—often interconnected—reasons include:

○ **Caring.** At its core, philanthropy is about caring. A private foundation is a very powerful way to convert caring into financial and related support for worthy causes. You need to care deeply about some charitable causes to justify establishing and running a private foundation.

○ **Legacy.** Many people create private foundations to honor loved ones. They're effective in binding a family together around something they consider meaningful. Many times private foundations are part of the education of inheritors in helping them become wise philanthropists. You should probably want to create a legacy—of one kind or another— if you choose to create and maintain a private foundation.

○ **Permanence.** You can establish your private foundation in perpetuity. Consequently, you can ensure that the charitable institutions and causes that are important to you will continue to be funded indefinitely. The ability for your private foundation to last forever, if you so choose, is a very appealing characteristic to many affluent families.

While a private foundation can have tremendous benefits for the founders and family, there are other options. In particular, there's the donor advised fund.

PRIVATE FOUNDATIONS COMPARED TO DONOR ADVISED FUNDS

While there are a fair number of differences between donor advised funds and private foundations, to keep it simple we will distinguish them on three key measures—control, expenses, and family involvement including creating a legacy (Exhibit 15.1).

EXHIBIT 15.1: Donor Advised Funds vs. Foundations

CONSIDERATIONS	DONOR ADVISED FUND	PRIVATE FOUNDATION
Control	Make recommendations	Make decisions
Expenses	Minimal	Various
Family involvement and creating a legacy	Lower	Higher

Control. A private foundation gives you significant control, which is not the case with a donor-advised fund. With a donor advised fund, you're only making recommendations to a firm responsible for both managing and distributing the money. While it's often unlikely that your suggestions will not be followed, there are certainly times when this will be the case.

A private foundation enables you to make a wider array of grants than a donor advised fund. For example, with a donor advised fund you couldn't make pledge agreements. Therefore, you cannot say that over a period of time you'll support a charitable cause because you're not in control of the fund. With a private foundation, you can choose to make such agreements. Also private foundations can make grants to specific individuals; something a donor advised fund cannot accomplish.

How the assets are managed differs between the two. With a donor advised fund, the assets are managed by the firm you entrusted with your monies. In a private foundation, you or investment advisors you select are managing the assets.

All in all, private foundations can be much more creative in how they manage the endowment and how they give (see below). The same cannot be said of donor advised funds.

Expenses. Private foundations are generally a more costly proposition than a donor advised fund. Generally speaking, private foundations are required to annually give away a minimum of five percent of their assets. Currently, there are no annual giving requirements for donor advised funds.

Donor advised funds get greater tax deductions. They get 50 percent tax write-offs for cash donations and 30 percent write-offs for securities. In comparison, private foundations get a 30 percent deduction for cash and 20 percent deduction for securities.

The administrative costs of a donor advised fund are also less and the reporting requirements, for example, are not as extensive.

Family involvement and creating a legacy. In the case of a private foundation, there are unlimited succession possibilities. This enables the family to exercise control across generations. Many donor advised funds have limitations on successions. When that limit is reached, the monies go into a general pool at the sponsoring organization.

Where there's a strong interest in having your charitable giving live on after you, including permitting your descendants to take the reins, private foundations tend to be the more effective choice. You're able to decide who sits on the governing board and how funds are spent. In contrast, a board selected by the sponsoring organization governs the donor advised fund.

THE EVOLVING WORLD OF PRIVATE FOUNDATIONS

Like advanced planning, the world of private foundations is creatively developing. From innovative ways to support worthy causes to pioneering ways to invest their endowments, many private foundations are furthering their agendas in numerous meaningful ways. The intent is to start with a problem and then determine the best forms of support to help solve the problem. Many private foundations are seeing this as a necessity as they struggle to find effective and powerful ways to expand their social and environmental effectiveness.

Today, there are an increasingly wide variety of financial instruments and strategies being applied beyond traditional grant-making. Examples of this include loans, loan guarantees, bonds, and bond guarantees. We'll look at two trends gaining traction in the world of private foundations—creative use of philanthropic capital in the form of program-related investments and impact investing. The intent is to leverage limited resources to accomplish more.

Program-related investments were defined in the Tax Reform Act of 1969. They're provided to worthy causes, but unlike a grant, they may need to be repaid, usually with a below-market rate of return. While often structured as loans, program-related investments can also be loan guarantees, linked deposits, and even equity investments. This way, private foundations can more creatively use their endowment monies where strict grant-making is unsuitable or just not enough.

It's useful to understand that program-related investing isn't exactly new. Over 200 years ago, Benjamin Franklin started a charity with 2,000 pounds sterling to provide loans to indigent artisans.

Program-related investments are usually made only to not-for-profit organizations, but there are exceptions. For example, a program-related investment can be made to a profit-making corporation if that firm uses the funds for charitable activities such as building affordable housing in underserved areas.

Obtaining a program-related investment is often similar to obtaining a grant. However, there are some meaningful differences. Program-related investments generally require more information than grants. Overall, the more innovative the investment and the more complex the endeavor, the more information the private foundation will require.

Program-related investments tend to be more customized. They often don't fit the more systematic pattern associated with grant-making. This, in turn, many times leads to more extensive negotiations by the parties involved.

Impact investing is where private foundations are making investments into companies and funds with the objectives of getting a solid financial return and creating a discernable social and/or environmental impact. Both these objectives need to be pursued, as the belief is that the creation of economic value and social value can occur in partnership.

The objective is to employ market pressures to achieve social and environmental benefits to positively influence the behavior of corporations. The underlying logic is that by changing the behavior of these corporations in constructive ways, impact investors are reducing problems at the source rather than needing to help remedy problems after the fact.

Basically, there are two types of impact investors:

○ **Financial first investors** are looking to get the best financial return while also seeking to get a social and/or environmental impact. They want to meet a threshold of social and/or environmental impact while achieving, at a minimum, market rate returns.

○ **Impact first investors** are focused strongly on the social and/or environmental benefits they can generate. While they're interested in a financial return on their investment, they're willing to accept a range of returns usually from a return of principal to market rates, as long as other forms of impact are achieved.

The appeal of impact investing for private foundations is that they can pursue their philanthropic agendas with the monies they invest coupled with their grants (and potentially program-related investments).

There are many other ways private foundations are being increasingly creative. From issuing debt and leveraging commercial loans to working with co-funders such as other private foundations and family offices (see *Chapter 14: The Family Office Option*), private foundations are making significant strides all with the aim of creating a better world.

CONCLUSIONS

If your business success makes you very wealthy, and—like so many business owners—you're committed to giving back, you'll probably consider establishing and running your own private foundation. Doing so will enable you to support the charitable causes that are important to you and enable you to use the skills and talents that were instrumental to your business success for philanthropic purposes.

If a private foundation is not for you, there are other options such as a donor advised fund or the ability to leverage charitable trusts for both personal wealth creation and "doing good" (see *Chapter 8: Solving Problems*). What's most important is that you can be philanthropic in ways that best work for you.

Thomas F. Blaney, CPA, CFE, *is a partner of O'Connor Davies and the Co-Director of the Firm's Private Foundation Practice. With over 30 years of experience, Mr. Blaney is a recognized authority in his field and a frequently sought after speaker at national conferences. He has authored many Private Foundation Primers, covering topics ranging from governance to start-ups, which are widely distributed and referenced by foundations both large and small. Mr. Blaney provided leadership and insights in the initial technical review of the L3C Concept, a type of program-related investment with a for-profit element to investors, and was a member of the 990PF Rewrite Advisory Committee for Private Foundations.*

Christopher D. Petermann, CPA, *is a partner of O'Connor Davies and the Co-Director of the Firm's Private Foundation Practice. He has over 30 years of specialized experience in accounting and auditing for private foundations, and exempt organizations, as well as closely-held businesses and financial service entities.*

SEVEN INTERCONNECTED TRENDS

WITH
KEVIN J. KEANE

ooking to the future, it's easy to identify the critical relationship between successful business owners and advanced planning. As there are a number of fairly solid structural patterns in place, as advanced planning is, by its nature, oriented toward the future, and as business owners have certain psychological-rational consistencies, we see the following seven interconnected trends:

1 **Successful businesses will continue to be the most likely way to create significant personal wealth**. Equity ownership has historically been the primary source and driver of personal wealth creation. In our society, where the social structure continues to be defined and refined by an amalgamation of laws and regulations, equity in a successful venture will remain the principal and dominant way to become affluent.

To create a substantial or even a moderate personal fortune, you will probably need to have equity in a business. As previously noted, ownership, per se, is not enough. Provided you're not simply an investor in the business, you'll also need to help move the business forward. To this end *Millionaire Intelligence* is probably instrumental.

IMPLICATION: *Your decision to be a business owner puts you squarely in the "line of money." It's potentially your passport to meaningful personal wealth.*

---

2 **A core motivation of most business owners will remain becoming wealthy.** With the multitude of risks and commitments required to make a business successful, and while there are many reasons people create and manage businesses, we find that the potential to become wealthy and possibly extremely wealthy is almost always fairly high on the agenda. Simply put, the desire for personal wealth is regularly characteristic of most business owners.

While personal wealth creation is a core motivation, this says nothing as to how the business owners intend to use their personal wealth. No doubt some affluent business owners will be hedonistic, but research shows that the majority will deploy their affluence in the service of their families as well as bettering some aspect of the world through philanthropy.

IMPLICATION: *As a business owner, desiring to become wealthy puts you in excellent company. In fact, if becoming wealthy is one of your motivations for being a business owner, you're much more likely to be able to join the ranks of the very well to do.*

3 **Death, taxes, and, litigants are constants.** Benjamin Franklin in a letter to Jean-Baptiste Leroy in 1789 pointed out the certainty of death and taxes. To these two constants we can add litigation as long as there's a court system. While death is unavoidable, the impact of taxes and the likelihood of litigation can often be mitigated.

Advanced planning, like most man-made contrivances, is largely useless when it comes to avoiding death, save for the fact that you can have more money for the finest medical care. However, advanced planning can be astoundingly effective in providing ways to legitimately lower taxes and protect you from unsubstantiated lawsuits.

IMPLICATION: *Successful business owners must deal with the consequences of taxes and the ongoing possibility of lawsuits, but you can limit the adverse effects of both with the expertise of a high-caliber advanced planner. Your aim, therefore, should be to ensure you are selecting and working with the highest-quality professional.*

4 **Wealth maximization will persistently be in demand.** Because it takes so much time, effort, and ingenuity to make a company successful and, in turn, generate enough income and value to make its owners rich, the desire to enhance and protect the wealth is likely to be an ongoing objective for business owners. Although there are other factors that may influence strategies and decisions, such as emotional attachments to people, places, and things and legal and moral obligations to partners and employees, the majority of business owners will remain focused on making the most of the wealth they have by minimizing taxes, investing wisely, and protecting it from litigants and creditors.

As noted throughout this primer, advanced planning is a time-tested, ethically sound methodology to achieve personal wealth maximization. It has been proven over and over again to enable business owners to legally maintain their wealth against those who desire to share it and even increase their wealth in certain circumstances.

IMPLICATION: *Working hard or harder to make money is admirable, but it's wise to ensure that the wealth you've already created is still there for you and your family when you need it. Advanced planning strategies enable you to do this and, thus, the need for this specialized discipline will remain as long as there are businesses.*

New advanced planning strategies will evolve. The legal and regulatory environments are constantly changing due to factors that are out of your control. Consequently, advanced planning strategies must be adaptable, and new strategies must be developed to help business owners, wealth holders, and financial professionals address and profit from these changes.

The Innovation Process is critical in order to develop solutions that maximize wealth in a changing legal and regulatory environment. Intellectual prowess directed through an ethical prism enables advanced planners to provide business owners new and inventive solutions.

IMPLICATION: *New advanced planning strategies will perpetually be generated, and it's your responsibility, in partnership with your team of professionals, to confirm that the options you've selected are up-to-date and still work in the context of current legal and regulatory parameters. Most importantly, you should always keep in mind that every advanced planning strategy you use must be morally validated.*

Financial predators and incompetents will multiply. As the competitive environment for professionals becomes increasingly difficult, if not out-and-out hostile, the appeal of business owners and their assets—which is already considerable—will only intensify. Among these financial and legal professionals are those who look to take advantage. Aside from the financial predators, there is a plethora of well meaning but technically limited professionals.

Many financial predators will become more poised and polished making it complicated to discern their malicious intent. At the same time, the number of incompetents will compound due to delusion and denial, and a great many of them will focus on business owners out of financial necessity.

IMPLICATION: *You can lose your fortune and possibly your liberty by entrusting your monies and your business to unscrupulous or hopelessly ineffective professionals. In all likelihood, as the number of such individuals is growing, you must make sure to choose your advanced planner carefully.*

7 **Success will continue to be a function of selecting and managing your advanced planner.** In the hands of a capable professional, advanced planning strategies can help business owners maximize their wealth while protecting it from unjust lawsuits.

The failures of advanced planning are not in the strategies, per se, but rather in the planners who design them. Most professionals holding themselves out as advanced planners are usually not up to the job or are looking to exploit uninformed business owners. A business owner's success using advanced planning strategies will continue to be predicated on the quality of the advanced planner chosen and the way the relationship is structured.

IMPLICATION: *Your ability to get the multitude of benefits that are possible using advanced planning strategies is only possible when you take an active role in sourcing and working with a high-caliber advanced planner. It's your wealth; it's your future and the future of your loved ones; it's your responsibility.*

If you sum it up, these seven interconnected trends demonstrate the ongoing value advanced planning has for business owners as they build their wealth and then turn their attention to managing and protecting it. It's also exceedingly evident that the proficiencies and the ethical orientation of the advanced planner with whom you decide to work will dramatically impact your ability to judiciously maximize your wealth.

It's worth repeating:

When it comes to advanced planning, your most important decisions are the caliber of the professionals with whom you choose to work and how you manage those relationships.

Kevin J. Keane, CPA, is the Managing Partner of O'Connor Davies. He has more than 30 years of experience providing accounting, auditing, and business advisory services to family businesses in the manufacturing, distribution, real estate, and construction industries.

APPENDICES

APPENDIX A
SURVEY OF BUSINESS OWNERS

In 2014, we conducted a survey of 513 business owners. Each respondent had to meet the following criteria in order to be included in the study:

○ Each business represented had to be privately held.

○ Each business represented had to be in continuous operation for at least five years.

○ Each business represented had to have minimum average annual revenues of $1 million or more in both of the preceding two years.

○ Each business owner had to have a minimum equity stake of 20 percent in the company.

KEY DEMOGRAPHICS

The survey respondents represent a wide range of industries (Exhibit A.1). The largest group of business owners, at 39 percent, has service-oriented operations. Retail and wholesale businesses were the next largest group at 19 percent, followed by real estate and construction companies at 14 percent. Manufacturing and distribution rounded out the top five fields at 12 percent and 10 percent respectively.

EXHIBIT A.1:
Business Types
% N = 513 BUSINESS OWNERS

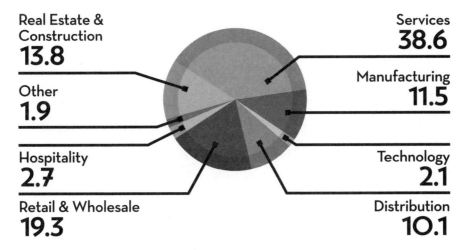

Real Estate & Construction
13.8

Services
38.6

Other
1.9

Manufacturing
11.5

Hospitality
2.7

Technology
2.1

Retail & Wholesale
19.3

Distribution
10.1

The majority of business owners surveyed, about 44 percent, represented companies that generate average annual revenues between $5 million and $10 million per year (Exhibit A.2). The next largest segment, or 22 percent, represented companies with revenues between $10 million and $50 million. Another way to look at it is that 18 percent of respondents were from companies generating less than $5 million, while the 82 percent represented companies with revenues in excess of that. At the other end of the spectrum, 39 percent of respondents represented companies with average annual revenues in excess of $10 million.

EXHIBIT A.2:
Average Annual Revenues in the Previous 2 Years
% N = 513 BUSINESS OWNERS

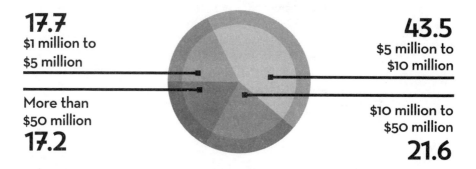

17.7
$1 million to
$5 million

43.5
$5 million to
$10 million

More than
$50 million
17.2

$10 million to
$50 million
21.6

Four out of five of the business owners surveyed had equity partners in their enterprises, a common situation that has many implications for the advanced planning process and the ability to maximize personal wealth derived from ownership stakes (Exhibit A.3).

EXHIBIT A.3:
Equity Partners
% N = 513 BUSINESS OWNERS

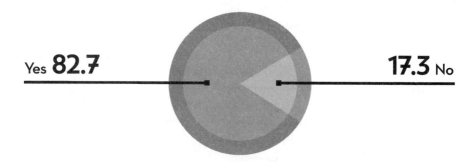

Yes **82.7**

17.3 No

Nearly two-thirds of the business owners answering the survey were between the ages of 40 years old and 55 years old (Exhibit A.4). Almost a fifth of the business owners were older than 55 with the remaining business owners younger than 40 years old.

EXHIBIT A.4:

Age of Owner Answering the Survey
% N = 513 BUSINESS OWNERS

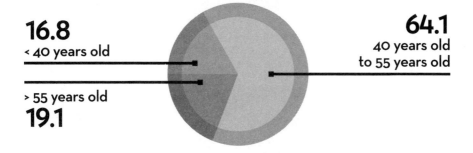

16.8
< 40 years old

64.1
40 years old
to 55 years old

> 55 years old
19.1

APPENDIX B
MAXIMIZING PERSONAL WEALTH WHEN SELLING YOUR BUSINESS
With Ronald F. DeSoiza and Thomas Sorrentino

Selling their business is on the minds of nearly nine out of ten of the business owners surveyed (Exhibit B.1). The reasons vary, but it remains a key focus for new and established proprietors. The high positive response rate does not mean they're planning to sell in the near future or that they have a specific buyer in mind, but rather that the idea of selling is a serious consideration, which must be fully explored.

EXHIBIT B.1:

Interested in One Day Selling the Business
% N = 513 BUSINESS OWNERS

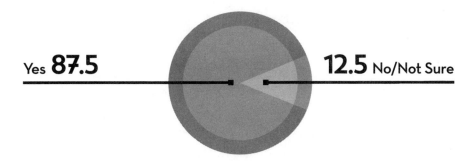

Yes **87.5**   **12.5** No/Not Sure

Despite the implied level of enthusiasm for selling, just a third of the business owners say they've tracked the sales activities of other business owners in order to understand the process and evaluate the results (Exhibit B.2). The overarching impression among them is that about half of sellers are dissatisfied with their post-sale results, especially the financial results which include the valuation, the agreed-upon sales price, the associated tax hit, and the residual proceeds. In balance, it is the view of these business owners that about a third of sellers are satisfied and just 12 percent are highly satisfied (Exhibit B.3).

EXHIBIT B.2:

Know a Business Owner Who Sold His/Her Company
% N = 513 BUSINESS OWNERS

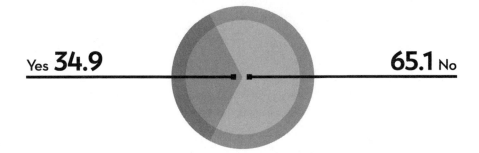

Yes **34.9**   **65.1** No

EXHIBIT B.3:

General Overall Perception of the Results
% N = 179 BUSINESS OWNERS

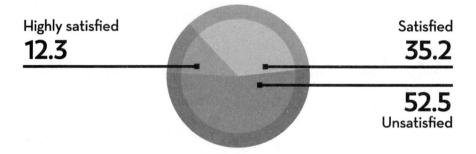

Highly satisfied
12.3

Satisfied
35.2

52.5
Unsatisfied

As we're considering the views of people a few degrees away from the sale itself, there are a multitude of complications in interpreting these findings. Nevertheless, these results match up with other research on business owners selling their companies, our own experiences, and that of other professionals in the field. Without question, many business owners are ultimately unhappy with the results from the sale of their biggest asset: their companies.

It's also important to realize that post-sale satisfaction levels can be influenced by a variety of factors which may not be financial in nature nor within the seller's control, such as the timeliness and transparency of the process, how well or realistically the expectations were set in advance, the expertise and profes-sionalism of the advisors, interactions and negotiations with the new owners, and the future structure and direction of the company. That is why it's essential for all business owners to understand where and how they can have the great-est impact on the future value of their business and their own personal wealth.

If you're going to sell your business, you're probably looking to make sure you derive the greatest financial benefit possible. Of course, there can be mitigating circumstances such as family and business partner considerations that can create emotional and organizational encumbrances. However, getting the most for your company when you sell is typically a key goal of business owners. While this singular objective is pervasive and can be all consuming, it tends to be a little short sighted.

In order to get the best personal financial results from the sale of your business, smart pre-sale planning is essential. When pre-sale planning is coupled with astute negotiation (see *Chapter 3: Bargaining Brilliance*), it generally results in securing the best price for your company and also allows you to retain the maximum amount of money from the transaction (Exhibit B.4).

EXHIBIT B.4:

Putting the Most Money in Your Pocket

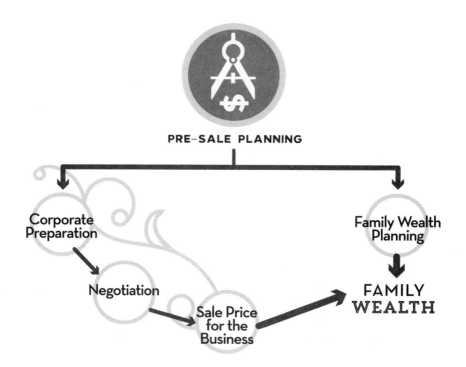

LACK OF PREPARATION CAN UNDERMINE VALUE

There are two types of pre-sale planning that can be significantly beneficial to business owners: corporate preparation and advanced planning.

Corporate preparation activities involve organizing a company for a sale. It includes efforts that will address any lingering operational or procedural problems that can impact profits, making sure that a proper infrastructure is in place along with the appropriate documentation, among other things. There are a variety of actions business owners can take to prepare their companies in order to command the best price. Unfortunately, among the business owners surveyed, very few have taken any of these steps to strengthen and secure their financial future (Exhibit B.5).

EXHIBIT B.5:
Pre-Sale Corporate Actions
% N = 449 BUSINESS OWNERS

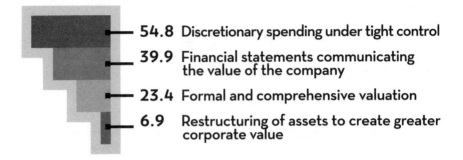

54.8 Discretionary spending under tight control

39.9 Financial statements communicating the value of the company

23.4 Formal and comprehensive valuation

6.9 Restructuring of assets to create greater corporate value

Corporate preparation can help increase the price business owners receive for their companies and can include a broad array of possible activities. Some of the most common and impactful are:

○ **Improving the balance sheet.** From doing a more effective job with cash management and accounts receivables to expunging non-performing assets and personnel, a company can effectively better its financials.

○ **Addressing the cost of funds.** The right loan covenants, for example, can make a significant difference when selling a company. The overall intent is to maximize the working capital arrangements.

○ **Enhancing profits.** Business owners should look to take a variety of steps, such as eliminating "bad" customers and refining operations, thereby increasing gross profit margins.

Another element of corporate preparation is "valuation." In most cases, a formal valuation is required for the ownership transfer of a business, regardless of whether the transition occurs between family members, within the current employee base, or to an outside individual or corporate entity.

If you want a formal valuation, you need to engage a qualified business appraiser who possesses specialized licenses and designations in valuation like the Accredited in Business Valuation (ABV) certification from the American Institute of Certified Public Accountants or the Accredited Senior Appraiser (ASA) certification from the American Society of Appraisers.

There are usually three approaches used to value a company:

○ The *income approach* uses the present value of expected future cash flows or operating income.

- The *market approach* is based on comparisons with similar companies where the value of these other firms is known.

- The *asset approach* is based on getting a fair market value of the business assets and then subtracting the fair market value of its liabilities.

One or more of these approaches may be used in the formal valuation process; your appraiser will determine which methods are most appropriate based on the nature of your business and its assets among other considerations. In addition to providing you with a baseline understanding of your company's perceived and expected value in the marketplace, the process of obtaining a formal valuation can often help you identify other ways to bolster value and, ultimately, the price a buyer is willing to pay.

Corporate preparation helps companies function better and appeals to potential suitors, but it is the ability to capitalize on these improvements during negotiations that translates into a higher sales price. The sales price itself, along with the accompanying terms and conditions, primarily accounts for the amount of personal wealth created.

Planning to make the company more attractive to prospective buyers is wise, but so is planning to ensure you get the greatest advantage on the back-end. Thus, this the importance of advanced planning.

Advanced planning can be extremely powerful in mitigating the taxes owed on the sale of your company. However, of the business owners interested in a possible sale of their companies, only about 15 percent have taken action to maximize their personal wealth or the wealth of their loved ones from a sale (Exhibit B.6).

EXHIBIT B.6:

Have Taken Action to Mitigate Taxes Owed on the Sale of Their Companies

% N = 449 BUSINESS OWNERS

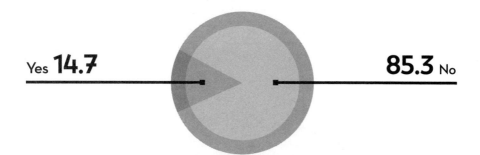

Yes **14.7**   **85.3** No

To get the most benefit from some advanced planning strategies, such as freezing the value of a business for estate planning purposes, you need to take action well before the sale. On the other hand, there are other advanced planning strategies that can be quite useful close to the transaction, such as using a charitable trust during the sale of all or part of the company (see *Chapter 8: Solving Problems*).

IMPLICATIONS

Selling your company is one of the most significant business decisions you're likely to make. It will probably have an enormous impact on your personal and financial life. Therefore, it's crucial that you take all the right actions to get the best possible outcome.

If you want to get the highest value for your company and retain as much as possible from the proceeds for personal, estate planning, or philanthropic purposes, pre-sale planning is essential. Failing to do so can prove heartbreaking later on.

Corporate preparation in conjunction with skilled negotiations can better enable you to get the best price for your company. Meanwhile, by taking advantage of various advanced planning strategies, you can dramatically lessen the potential tax bite now and in the future.

Ronald DeSoiza, CPA, BV, is a partner of O'Connor Davies and has more than 30 years of audit and accounting experience with regional and national firms. He also provides specialized services in succession planning, business valuation, litigation support, and taxation. In addition to his role as one of the Firm's audit partners in its commercial practice, he conducts peer reviews of CPA firms on behalf of the American Institute of Certified Public Accountants.

Thomas Sorrentino, CPA is a partner of O'Connor Davies with over 30 years of experience in public accounting. He provides audit, financial accounting and advisory services to business owners and executives, entrepreneurs and companies, including both public and privately-held organizations, in the commercial and real estate sectors.

ABOUT THE AUTHORS

RUSS ALAN PRINCE is the president of R. A. Prince & Associates, Inc., a globally-recognized research and consulting firm specializing in the creation and management of private wealth. He consults with business stakeholders and select professionals to strategically expand their networks to maximize the value of their relationships. Prince is a co-founder and the executive director of *Private Wealth* magazine and writes the *Serious Money* blog for Forbes. **www.russalanprince.com**

HANNAH SHAW GROVE is an expert on private wealth and business development, leveraging her in-depth understanding to counsel professionals and their companies on how to increase effectiveness with wealthy clients and attract more high-net-worth business. She is the author of 10 books and dozens of reports and articles that represent her empirical, theoretical and anecdotal findings, and a founder of *Private Wealth* magazine. **www.hsgrove.com**

CARLO A. SCISSURA. ESQ. is the President and CEO of the Brooklyn Chamber of Commerce. In this role, he leads one of New York's largest business advocacy and economic development organizations with nearly 2,000 members. Scissura has devoted much of his career to civil service and community improvement having served as General Counsel and Chief of Staff to the Brooklyn Borough President and served on the staffs of both a State Senator and an Assemblyman. Throughout his career, he has been appointed to a number of educational councils and served on the 2010 New York City Charter Commission, the New York City Economic Development Corporation, the Brooklyn Navy Yard Development Corporation, the Brooklyn Public Library, and is the President of the Federation of Italian-American Organizations.

FRANK W. SENECO is President of Seneco & Associates, Inc., one the leading advanced planning firms with a specialty in structuring sophisticated life insurance solutions. In conjunction with his partners, staff, and retained network of specialists, he works extensively with business owners to enhance their wealth, tax-efficiently transfer it to the next generation, and protect it from unjust lawsuits. Seneco speaks and writes frequently on these topics for the industry and is a co-author of the book *Protecting the Family Fortune: Advanced Planning for Ultra-High-Net-Worth Businesses* (2008). Seneco is a Principal and on the Board of Directors of the nationally recognized producer group, First Financial Resources. **www.seneco.com**

ABOUT THE PARTNERS

Brooklyn Chamber of Commerce

www.ibrooklyn.com

Founded in 1918, the **Brooklyn Chamber of Commerce** is the foremost resource for doing business within the borough. The Chamber promotes economic development and serves as an advocate for member businesses. It is respected as a leader in advancing public policy, new technologies, products, services, and programs that support and promote a healthy and vibrant local economy.

O'CONNOR DAVIES

PKF An Independant Member of PKF International

www.odpkf.com

O'Connor Davies, LLP is a full service Certified Public Accounting and consulting firm that has a long history of serving domestic and international clients and providing specialized professional services of the highest quality in a timely and cost-effective fashion. With roots tracing to 1891, the firm provides a complete range of accounting, auditing, tax, and management advisory services via its eight offices throughout New York, New Jersey, and Connecticut and more than 500 professionals. O'Connor Davies is recognized by its peers and is regularly included in annual rankings by trade journals *Accounting Today* and *INSIDE Public Accounting*. The firm is member of PKF International, a network of legally independent firms providing accounting and business advisory services in 440 locations in over 125 countries around the world.

$\mathscr{P}$rivate Wealth

www.pw-mag.com

Private Wealth is the leading media resource for wealth advisors, family offices, and elite practitioners that serve the needs of the ultra-high-net-worth markets. Its subscribers are gatekeepers and influencers to the world's wealthiest individuals and collectively represent tremendous purchasing power. Through a combination of print and digital publications, webinars, workshops, conferences, and thought leadership offerings, qualified professionals get access to timely, sophisticated editorial coverage of the financial, legal, insurance and risk management, advanced planning, and lifestyle issues that face today's wealth-holders and their families.

Forbes

www.forbes.com/sites/russalanprince/

The *Serious Money* blog on **Forbes.com** is dedicated to providing timely, research-based and empirical insights into the creation and management of exceptional wealth. Each post showcases the views and experiences of leading specialists and experts to the financial elite and regularly covers critical topics such as business ownership, self-made millionaires, *Millionaire Intelligence*, wealth-creating behaviors, negotiation tactics, family offices, philanthropy, and best practices.